At Issue

Embryonic and
Adult Stem Cells

Other Books in the At Issue Series:

At Issue

Embryonic and Adult Stem Cells

Margaret Haerens, Book Editor

GREENHAVEN PRESS
A part of Gale, Cengage Learning

GALE
CENGAGE Learning™

Detroit • New York • San Francisco • New Haven, Conn • Waterville, Maine • London

GALE
CENGAGE Learning

Christine Nasso, *Publisher*
Elizabeth Des Chenes, *Managing Editor*

© 2009 Greenhaven Press, a part of Gale, Cengage Learning.

Gale and Greenhaven Press are registered trademarks used herein under license.

For more information, contact:
Greenhaven Press
27500 Drake Rd.
Farmington Hills, MI 48331-3535
Or you can visit our Internet site at gale.cengage.com

For product information and technology assistance, contact us at

Gale Customer Support, 1-800-877-4253
For permission to use material from this text or product, submit all requests online at www.cengage.com/permissions

Further permissions questions can be emailed to permissionrequest@cengage.com

Articles in Greenhaven Press anthologies are often edited for length to meet page requirements. In addition, original titles of these works are changed to clearly present the main thesis and to explicitly indicate the author's opinion. Every effort is made to ensure that Greenhaven Press accurately reflects the original intent of the authors. Every effort has been made to trace the owners of copyrighted material.

Cover image © Images.com/Corbis.

LIBRARY OF CONGRESS CATALOGING-IN-PUBLICATION DATA

Embryonic and Adult Stem Cells / Margaret Haerens, book editor.
   p. cm. -- (At issue)
  Includes bibliographical references and index.
  ISBN 978-0-7377-4282-4 (hardcover)
  ISBN 978-0-7377-4281-7 (pbk.)
  1. Stem cells--Research. 2. Embryonic stem cells--Research. 3. Stem cells--Social aspects. 4. Research--Finance. 5. Science and state. I. Haerens, Margaret.
  QH588.S83E45 2009
  616'.02774--dc22

                                   2008051757

Printed in the United States of America
1 2 3 4 5 6 7 13 12 11 10 09

Contents

Introduction

On July 18, 2006, the U.S. Senate voted to approve a bill that would lift restrictions on federally funded embryonic stem cell research. Already passed by the House of Representatives, the Stem Cell Research Enhancement Act reflected the will of the American people, who had shown support for federal funding for embryonic stem cell research in poll after poll. The bill aimed to expand the number of embryonic stem-cell lines eligible for federal research funds—from the twenty-one lines President George W. Bush had designated in 2001 to numerous additional stem-cell lines derived from unwanted and unused embryos donated by in vitro fertilization clinics. According to the bill, women donating the embryos would have to provide written consent and could not receive a financial reward or other inducement.

A day later, however, President Bush vetoed the bill—rejecting Congress's bid to lift funding restrictions on human embryonic stem cell research and issuing the first veto of his five-year-old administration.

Surrounded by children developed from frozen embryos, President Bush explained his veto to the American public:

> Like all Americans, I believe our nation must vigorously pursue the tremendous possibility that science offers to cure disease and improve the lives of millions. We have opportunities to discover cures and treatments that were unthinkable generations ago. Some scientists believe that one source of these cures might be embryonic stem cell research. Embryonic stem cells have the ability to grow into specialized adult tissues, and this may give them the potential to replace damaged or defective cells or body parts and treat a variety of diseases.

> Yet we must also remember that embryonic stem cells come from human embryos that are destroyed for their cells. Each

of these human embryos is a unique human life with inherent dignity and matchless value. We see that value in the children who are with us today. Each of these children began his or her life as a frozen embryo that was created for in vitro fertilization, but remained unused after the fertility treatments were complete. Each of these children was adopted while still an embryo, and has been blessed with the chance to grow up in a loving family. These boys and girls are not spare parts. They remind us of what is lost when embryos are destroyed in the name of research. They remind us that we all begin our lives as a small collection of cells. And they remind us that in our zeal for new treatments and cures, America must never abandon our fundamental morals.

In June 2007, the Congress once again tried to pass a version of the Stem Cell Research Enhancement Act. President Bush vetoed the bill on June 20, 2007, framing embryonic stem cell research as a moral issue intimately connected to the question of when life begins. "I believe this [bill] will encourage taxpayer money to be spent on the destruction or endangerment of living human embryos," Bush said in a statement. The president also issued an executive order that encouraged scientists to develop new methods to obtain stem cells without harming human embryos. Supporters of the bill could not muster enough votes to override the president's veto.

These events underscore the controversial nature of the stem cell debate in the United States. The tension between scientific progress that holds the promise of relieving human suffering and the ethical and moral conundrum of destroying embryonic stem cells—and therefore potential human life—has been a burning political concern in the United States for the past decade.

For supporters of federal funding for embryonic stem cell research, the aim of finding cures for diseases such as Parkinson's, diabetes, cancer, Alzheimer's, heart disease, and spinal cord injuries is enough to overcome any ethical misgiv-

ings they may have about research on embryonic stem cells that would have been disposed of anyway. Relieving human suffering is a strong incentive, and scientists agree that embryonic stem cell research is one of the brightest hopes to make significant medical breakthroughs in fighting such debilitating diseases.

For opponents, federal funding of stem cell research condones the destruction of viable embryos that could develop into healthy, productive human beings. To be pro-life means to protect life at all stages, including embryos, they declare. Therefore, opponents urge the funding and development of other forms of stem cell research—particularly that on adult stem cells. They believe that government funding of adult stem cell research avoids the ethical and moral controversies surrounding the development of embryonic stem cell research while still providing solid progress in scientific and medical research.

Federal funding of embryonic stem cell research has been a controversial issue for the past decade. Politicians have used it as a hot-button issue to garner support or to paint their opponents as immoral, unethical, or callous to the plight of the suffering. The viewpoints presented in this volume explore the various perspectives in this long-standing debate and chronicle the scientific progress that has resulted from stem cell research in recent years.

1

Stem Cells: An Overview

The National Academies

The National Academies include three prestigious societies—the National Academy of Sciences, the National Academy of Engineering, and the Institute of Medicine—as well as the National Research Council. The National Academies solicit committees of America's top scientists, engineers, and other experts, to study difficult and important issues.

The discovery of stem cells in the 1950s allowed scientists to investigate a real potential for human regeneration for the first time. Embryonic and adult stem cells have demonstrated different functional limitations and social acceptability, but both offer progressive possibilities for medical research. The debates over stem cells have attempted to answer questions of ethical implications and will continue to do so as the research advances.

For centuries, scientists have known that certain animals can regenerate missing parts of their bodies. Humans actually share this ability with animals like the starfish and the newt. Although we can't replace a missing leg or a finger, our bodies are constantly regenerating blood, skin, and other tissues. The identity of the powerful cells that allow us to regenerate some tissues was first revealed when experiments with bone marrow in the 1950s established the existence of *stem cells* in our bodies and led to the development of bone marrow transplantation, a therapy now widely used in medicine.

This discovery raised hope in the medical potential of regeneration. For the first time in history, it became possible for physicians to regenerate a damaged tissue with a new supply of healthy cells by drawing on the unique ability of stem cells to create many of the body's specialized cell types.

Once they had recognized the medical potential of regeneration through the success of bone marrow transplants, scientists sought to identify similar cells within the embryo. Early studies of human development had demonstrated that the cells of the embryo were capable of producing every cell type in the human body. Scientists were able to extract embryonic stem cells from mice in the 1980s, but it wasn't until 1998 that a team of scientists from the University of Wisconsin–Madison became the first group to isolate human embryonic stem cells and keep them alive in the laboratory. The team knew that they had in fact isolated stem cells because the cells could remain unspecialized for long periods of time, yet maintained the ability to transform into a variety of specialized cell types, including nerve, gut, muscle, bone, and cartilage cells.

All stem cells may prove useful for medical research, but each of the different types has both promise and limitations.

Stem cell research is being pursued in the hope of achieving major medical breakthroughs. Scientists are striving to create therapies that rebuild or replace damaged cells with tissues grown from stem cells and offer hope to people suffering from cancer, diabetes, cardiovascular disease, spinal-cord injuries, and many other disorders. Both adult and embryonic stem cells may also provide a route for scientists to develop valuable new methods of drug discovery and testing. They are also powerful tools for doing the research that leads to a bet-

ter understanding of the basic biology of the human body. By drawing on expert scientists, doctors, bioethicists, and others, the National Academies have examined the potential of stem cell technologies for medicine and provided a forum for discussing the ethical implications and moral dilemmas of stem cell research.

What Is a Stem Cell?

Ultimately, every cell in the human body can be traced back to a fertilized egg that came into existence from the union of egg and sperm. But the body is made up of over 200 different types of cells, not just one. All of these cell types come from a pool of *stem cells* in the early embryo. During early development, as well as later in life, various types of stem cells give rise to the *specialized* or *differentiated* cells that carry out the specific functions of the body, such as skin, blood, muscle, and nerve cells.

Over the past two decades, scientists have been gradually deciphering the processes by which unspecialized stem cells become the many specialized cell types in the body. Stem cells can regenerate themselves or produce specialized cell types. This property makes stem cell appealing for scientists seeking to create medical treatments that replace lost or damaged cells.

Stem cells are found in all of us, from the early stages of human development to the end of life. All stem cells may prove useful for medical research, but each of the different types has both promise and limitations. Embryonic stem cells, which can be derived from a very early stage in human development, have the potential to produce all of the body's cell types. Adult stem cells, which are found in certain tissues in fully developed humans, from babies to adults, may be limited to producing only certain types of specialized cells. Recently,

scientists have also identified stem cells in umbilical cord blood and the placenta that can give rise to the various types of blood cells. . . .

Embryonic Stem Cells

A *blastocyst* (BLAST-oh-sist), is a pre-implantation embryo that develops 5 days after the fertilization of an egg by a sperm. It contains all the material necessary for the development of a complete human being. The blastocyst is a mostly hollow sphere of cells that is smaller than the period at the end of this sentence. In its interior is the inner cell mass, which is composed of 30–40 cells that are referred to by scientists as *pluripotent* because they can differentiate into all of the cell types of the body. In common usage, "embryo" can refer to all stages of development from fertilization until a somewhat ill-defined stage when it is called a fetus. Scientists use terms such as "morula" and "blastocyst" to refer to precise, specific stages of pre-implantation development. In order to be as precise as possible, this [viewpoint] uses the scientific terms when describing scientific concepts but uses the term "embryo" where more precision seemed likely to confuse rather than clarify.

In normal development, the blastocyst would implant in the wall of the uterus to become the embryo and continue developing into a mature organism. Its outer cells would begin to form the placenta and the inner cell mass would begin to differentiate into the progressively more specialized cell types of the body.

When the blastocyst is used for stem cell research, scientists remove the inner cell mass and place these cells in a culture dish with a nutrient-rich liquid where they give rise to embryonic stem cells. Embryonic stem cells seem to be more flexible than stem cells found in adults, because they have the

potential to produce every cell type in the human body. They are also generally easier to collect, purify and maintain in the laboratory than adult stem cells.

Advantages

Scientists can induce embryonic stem cells to replicate themselves in an *undifferentiated* state for very long periods of time before stimulating them to create specialized cells. This means that just a few embryonic stem cells can build a large bank of stem cells to be used in experiments. However, such undifferentiated stem cells could not be used directly for tissue transplants because they can cause a type of tumor called a teratoma. To be used for therapies, embryonic stem cells would first need to be differentiated into specialized cell types.

Some find embryonic stem cell research to be morally objectionable, because when scientists remove the inner cell mass, the blastocyst no longer has the potential to become a fully developed human being.

The process called nuclear transfer *offers another potential way to produce embryonic stem cells.*

Sources

In Vitro Fertilization: The largest potential source of blastocysts for stem cell research is from in vitro fertilization (IVF) clinics. The process of IVF requires the retrieval of a woman's eggs via a surgical procedure after undergoing an intensive regimen of "fertility drugs," which stimulate her ovaries to produce multiple mature eggs. When IVF is used for reproductive purposes, doctors typically fertilize all of the donated eggs in order to maximize their chance of producing a viable blastocyst that can be implanted in the womb. Because not all the fertilized eggs are implanted, this has resulted in a large bank of "excess" blastocysts that are currently stored in freez-

ers around the country. The blastocysts stored in IVF clinics could prove to be a major source of embryonic stem cells for use in medical research. However, because most of these blastocysts were created before the advent of stem cell research, most donors were not asked for their permission to use these left-over blastocysts for research.

The in vitro fertilization (IVF) technique could potentially also be used to produce blastocysts specifically for research purposes. This would facilitate the isolation of stem cells with specific genetic traits necessary for the study of particular diseases. For example, it may be possible to study the origins of an inherited disease like cystic fibrosis using stem cells made from egg and sperm donors who have this disease. The creation of stem cells specifically for research using IVF is, however, ethically problematic for some people because it involves intentionally creating a blastocyst that will never develop into a human being.

Nuclear Transfer: The process called *nuclear transfer* offers another potential way to produce embryonic stem cells. In animals, nuclear transfer has been accomplished by inserting the nucleus of an already differentiated adult cell—for example, a skin cell—into a donated egg that has had its nucleus removed. This egg, which now contains the genetic material of the skin cell, is then stimulated to form a blastocyst from which embryonic stem cells can be derived. The stem cells that are created in this way are therefore copies or "clones" of the original adult cell because their nuclear DNA matches that of the adult cell.

As of the summer of 2006, nuclear transfer has not been successful in the production of human embryonic stem cells, but progress in animal research suggests that scientists may be able to use this technique to develop human stem cells in the future.

Scientists believe that if they are able to use nuclear transfer to derive human stem cells, it could allow them to study

the development and progression of specific diseases by creating stem cells containing the genes responsible for certain disorders. In the future, scientists may also be able to create "personalized" stem cells that contain only the DNA of a specific patient. The embryonic stem cells created by nuclear transfer would be genetically matched to a person needing a transplant, making it far less likely that the patient's body would reject the new cells than it would be with traditional tissue transplant procedures.

Although using nuclear transfer to produce stem cells is not the same as reproductive cloning, some are concerned about the potential misapplication of the technique for reproductive cloning purposes. Other ethical considerations include egg donation, which requires informed consent, and the possible destruction of blastocysts.

Adult Stem Cells

Adult stem cells are hidden deep within organs, surrounded by millions of ordinary cells, and may help replenish some of the body's cells when needed. In fact, some adult stem cells are currently being used in therapies. They have been found in several organs that need a constant supply of cells, such as the blood, skin, and lining of the gut, and have also been found in surprising places like the brain, which is not known to readily replenish its cells. Unlike embryonic stem cells, adult stem cells are already somewhat specialized. For example, blood stem cells normally only give rise to the many types of blood cells, and nerve stem cells can only make the various types of brain cells. Recent research however, suggests that some adult stem cells might be more flexible than previously thought, and may be made to produce a wider variety of cell types. For example, some experiments have suggested that blood stem cells isolated from adult mice may also be able to produce liver, muscle, and skin cells, but these results are not yet proven and have not been demonstrated with hu-

man cells. Nevertheless, scientists are working on finding a way to stimulate adult stem cells, or even other types of adult cells, to be more versatile. If they succeed, it could provide another source of unspecialized stem cells.

Ethical Implications

Scientists and society as a whole must consider the ethical implications of stem cell research. . . . Different ethical issues are raised by the wide range of stem cell research activities. In 2005, the National Academies published guidelines for scientists who do research with human embryonic stem cells to encourage responsible and ethically sensitive conduct in their work. Although the guidelines are not expressly legally binding, many researchers have voluntarily adopted them as a guide to what constitutes appropriate conduct in human embryonic stem cell research. Yet for some people, such guidelines are inadequate because they aim to govern a practice that they see as intrinsically unethical.

Although cloning and stem cell research are often lumped together in the context of ethical debates, the goals and results of the two are very different.

As the science advances, it is essential that scientists; religous, moral, and political leaders; and society as a whole continue to evaluate and communicate about the ethical implications of stem cell research.

The controversy over embryonic stem cell research touches on some of the same fundamental questions that society has grappled with in the debates over contraception, abortion, and in vitro fertilization. The questions at the center of the controversy concern the nature of early human life and the legal and moral status of the human embryo. Embryonic stem cell research often involves removing the inner cell mass from "excess" blastocysts that are unneeded by couples who have

completed their fertility treatment. This prevents those blasto-cysts from continuing to develop. Although such blastocysts would likely be discarded (and thus destroyed) by the clinics in any case, some believe that this does not make it morally acceptable to use them for research or therapeutic purposes. They believe that the life of a human being begins at the mo-ment of conception and that society undermines a commit-ment to human equality and to the protection of vulnerable individuals if blastocysts are used for such purposes. Some cultures and religious traditions oppose the use of human life as a means to some other end, no matter how noble that end might be. Other traditions support embryonic stem cell re-search because they believe that the embryo gains the moral status of a human being only after a few weeks or months of development. Many traditions emphasize obligations to heal the sick and ease suffering—goals for which embryonic stem cell research holds great potential—and favor embryonic stem cell research for this reason. Several religious groups are cur-rently involved in internal discussions about the status of the human embryo and have not yet established official opinions on the matter. Public opinion polls suggest that the majority of both religious and non-religious Americans support em-bryonic stem cell research, although public opinion seems di-vided about the creation or use of human blastocysts solely for research.

Reproductive Cloning

Although cloning and stem cell research are often lumped to-gether in the context of ethical debates, the goals and results of the two are very different. The common factor between current attempts at reproductive cloning and stem cell re-search is a laboratory technique called *nuclear transfer.* Using nuclear transfer, scientists can create blastocysts containing stem cells that are "clones" of a single adult cell by inserting the genetic material from an adult cell (for example, a skin

cell) into an egg whose nucleus has been removed. Scientists hope that they could derive stem cells from the cells inside such blastocysts and grow replacement tissues that are genetically matched to specific patients, thus offering patients a safer alternative to traditional tissue transplants.

Reproductive cloning, such as the process that was used to create Dolly the sheep [the first animal to be cloned, in 1996], also uses the nuclear transfer technique. However, instead of removing the inner cell mass to derive a stem cell line, the blastocyst is implanted into the uterus and allowed to develop fully. In 2002, the National Academies issued the report *Scientific and Medical Aspects of Human Reproductive Cloning*, which concluded "Human reproductive cloning should not now be practiced. It is dangerous and likely to fail."

The Ethics of Chimeras

Chimeras are organisms composed of cells or tissues from more than one individual. Chimeras have been produced for research for many years, but when human and animal cells are mixed in the laboratory, there is a clear need for heightened ethical consideration. Cells from different organisms can be combined either in the early developmental stages (for example, introducing human cells into a mouse blastocyst to observe certain developmental processes) or after an individual is fully developed (for example, implanting human stem cell–derived pancreatic cells into a mouse to test their ability to function in a living body). Chimeras are considered essential for advancing stem cell research to viable therapies, since no therapy can be tested in humans without research in animals first.

Some people believe that the creation of chimeras involving human cells for medical research is morally acceptable as long as the chimera has no level of human consciousness. Therefore, research in which it is possible for human stem cells to produce part of an animal's brain should be con-

ducted with great care. The National Academies' guidelines prohibit the introduction of human cells into the blastocyst of a non-human primate, or the introduction of any animal or human cells into a human blastocyst. The guidelines also prohibit the breeding of human-animal chimeras in the unlikely event that any human genetic material would be contained in their reproductive cells.

Embryonic Stem Cell Research Is Immoral

Mona Charen

Mona Charen is a political pundit, a nationally syndicated columnist, and the author of two best-selling books, Useful Idiots: How Liberals Got It Wrong in the Cold War and Still Blame America First *and* Do-Gooders: How Liberals Harm Those They Claim to Help—and the Rest of Us.

Embryonic stem cell research destroys life. We can take steps to minimize the numbers of embryos wasted by fertility clinics as well as those dehumanized by science. If we do not take these steps, we will cross a moral line and reach a slippery slope.

Addressing the [2004] Democratic National Convention, Ron Reagan told the delegates that in the debate over funding research on embryonic stem cells, we face a choice between "the future and the past; between reason and ignorance; between true compassion and mere ideology." Not satisfied with that contrast, he elaborated that "a few of these folks (who oppose funding this research) are just grinding a political axe, and they should be ashamed of themselves."

It is Reagan who ought to be ashamed. As the mother of a 10-year-old with juvenile diabetes, I yearn more than most for breakthroughs in scientific research. My son takes between four and six shots of insulin daily and must test his blood sugar by pricking his finger the same number of times. This

Mona Charen, "Stem Cell Debate Is Misleading," *The Cabin.net*, August 24, 2004. www.thecabin.net. By permission Mona Charen and Creators Syndicate, Inc.

disease affects every major organ system in the body and places him in the high-risk category for more problems than I care to name. When he settles down to sleep at night, I can never be entirely sure that he won't slip into a coma from sudden low blood sugar. How happily I would take the disease upon myself if I could only spare him! So please don't lecture me about grinding a political axe.

Pro-lifers oppose embryonic stem cell research . . . because they hold life sacred at all stages of development.

Crossing a Moral Line

But like millions of others, I am troubled by the idea of embryonic stem cell research. It crosses a moral line that this society should be loath to cross. Taking the stem cells from human embryos kills them. Before turning to the arguments of the pro-research side, permit a word about the pro-life position. Too many pro-life activists, it seems to me, have argued this case on the wrong grounds. My inbox is full of missives about the scientific misfires that stem cell research has led to, as well as announcements that adult stem cells hold more promise.

This is neither an honest nor a productive line of argument. The reason pro-lifers oppose embryonic stem cell research is because they hold life sacred at all stages of development. They ought not to deny this or dress it up in a lab coat to give it greater palatability.

Proponents of embryonic stem cell research point out that some of the embryos currently sitting in freezers in fertility clinics around the world are going to be washed down the drain anyway—which surely kills them, and without any benefit to mankind. This is true. There are several answers to this. The first is that a society that truly honored each human life would take a different approach. Fertility clinics and the

couples who use them would understand the moral obligation not to create more embryos than they can reasonably expect to transfer to the mother's uterus. In cases where this was impossible, the embryos could be placed for adoption with other couples.

These are treacherous moral waters we're setting sail in, and those who hesitate ought not to be scorned as ignorant, uncompassionate or blinkered.

Unknown Usefulness

Once you begin to pull apart a human embryo and use its parts, you have thoroughly dehumanized it. You have justified taking one life to (speculatively) save another. Despite the rosy future painted by Ron Reagan and others, those of us who follow the field with avid interest have been disappointed by avenues of research that have failed, thus far, to pan out. Still, opponents of stem cell research should not argue that the research is going to be fruitless. No one knows.

While the idea of growing spare parts—say, spinal nerves for a paraplegic—in a Petri dish seems wonderful, it may not be possible to do so from embryonic stem cells. As the *Wall Street Journal* reported on Aug. 12, 2004, scientists have been frustrated by their inability to get stem cells to grow into endoderm, whereas they can coax them to become heart and nerve tissue.

"Scientists speculate," the *Journal* explained, "that might be because the embryo early on needs blood and nerve tissue to grow, while endoderm-based organs aren't needed until later." If we can use the stem cells of normal human embryos for research, by what logic would we shrink from allowing an embryo to reach a later stage of development in order to study better how endoderm forms?

These are treacherous moral waters we're setting sail in, and those who hesitate ought not to be scorned as ignorant, uncompassionate or blinkered.

Embryonic Stem Cell Research Is Not a Moral Dilemma

Michael Kinsley

Michael Kinsley is a political journalist and pundit and founding editor of the online newsmagazine Slate.

The use of embryonic stem cells should not be a moral dilemma. Since embryos are disposed of every day in fertility clinics, and very few people oppose that practice, it is illogical to argue that embryonic stem cell research is immoral because it kills a potential life. The debate is not relevant because the arguments of opponents of embryonic stem cells are uninformed and undeveloped.

The Issue of stem-cell research . . . is often described as a moral dilemma, but it simply is not. Or at least it is not the moral dilemma often used in media shorthand: the rights of the unborn versus the needs of people suffering from diseases that embryonic stem cells might cure. As one of those people myself (I have Parkinson's), I am not an objective analyst of what the U.S. government's continuing near-ban on stem-cell research is costing our society and the world. Naturally, I think it's costing too much. No other potential therapy—including adult stem cells—is nearly as promising for my ailment and others. Evaluate that as you wish.

Against this, you have the fact that embryonic stem cells are extracted from human embryos, killing them in the pro-

cess. If you believe that embryos a few days after conception have the same human rights as you or me, killing innocent embryos is obviously intolerable. But do opponents of stem-cell research really believe that? Stem cells test that belief, and sharpen the basic right-to-life question, in a way abortion never has.

The Fate of Embryos

Here's why: Stem cells used in medical research generally come from fertility clinics, which produce more embryos than they can use. This isn't an accident—it is essential to their mission of helping people to have babies. Often these are "test tube babies": the product of an egg fertilized in the lab and then implanted in a womb to develop until birth. Controversy about test-tube babies has all but disappeared. Vague science-fiction alarms have been crushed by the practical evidence, and potential political backlash, of grateful, happy parents.

The vast majority of people who oppose stem-cell research either haven't thought it through, or have thought it through and don't care.

In any particular case, fertility clinics try to produce more embryos than they intend to implant. Then—like the Yale admissions office (only more accurately)—they pick and choose among the candidates, looking for qualities that make for a better human being. If you don't get into Yale, you have to attend a different college. If the fertility clinic rejects you, you get flushed away—or maybe frozen until the day you can be discarded without controversy.

And fate isn't much kinder to the embryos that make this first cut. Usually several of them are implanted in the hope that one will survive. Or, to put it another way, in the hope that all but one will not survive. And fertility doctors do their ruthless best to make these hopes come true.

In short, if embryos are human beings with full human rights, fertility clinics are death camps—with a side order of cold-blooded eugenics. No one who truly believes in the humanity of embryos could possibly think otherwise.

And, by the way, when it comes to respecting the human dignity of microscopic embryos, nature—or God—is as cavalier as the most godless fertility clinic. The casual creation and destruction of embryos in normal human reproduction is one reason some people, like me, find it hard to make the necessary leap of faith to believe that an embryo and, say, [South African political hero] Nelson Mandela, are equal in the eyes of God.

Rethinking Stem-Cell Research

Proponents of stem-cell research like to emphasize that it doesn't cost the life of a single embryo. The embryos killed to extract their stem cells were doomed already. But this argument gives too much ground, and it misses the point. If embryos are human beings, it's not OK to kill them for their stem cells just because you were going to kill them, or knowingly let them die, anyway. The better point—the killer point, if you'll pardon the expression—is that if embryos are human beings, the routine practices of fertility clinics are far worse—both in numbers and in criminal intent—than stem-cell research. And yet no one objects, or objects very loudly. President [George W.] Bush actually praised the work of fertility clinics in his first speech announcing restrictions on stem cells.

Even strong believers in abortion rights (I'm one) ought to acknowledge and respect the moral sincerity of many right-to-lifers. I cannot share—or even fathom—their conviction that a microscopic dot—as oblivious as a rock, more primitive than a worm—has the same human rights as anyone reading this article. I don't have their problem with the question of when human life begins. (When did "human" life begin dur-

ing evolution? Obviously, there is no magic point. But that doesn't prevent us from claiming humanity for ourselves and denying it to the embryolike entities we evolved from.) Nevertheless, abortion opponents deserve respect for more than just their right to hold and express an opinion we disagree with. Excluding, of course, the small minority who believe that their righteousness puts them above the law, sincere right-to-lifers deserve respect as that rarity in modern American politics: a strong interest group defending the interest of someone other than themselves.

Or so I always thought—until the arrival of stem cells. Moral sincerity is not impressive if it depends on willful ignorance and indifference to logic. Not every stem-cell opponent deserves to have his or her debater's license taken away. There are a few, no doubt, who actually are as horrified by fertility clinics as they are by stem-cell research, and a subset of this subset may even be doing something about it. But these people, if they exist, are not a political force strong enough to stop a juggernaut of medical progress that so many other people are desperate to encourage. The vast majority of people who oppose stem-cell research either haven't thought it through, or have thought it through and don't care.

I wish they would think again.

The Government's Policy Regarding Stem Cell Research Is Contradictory

Michael J. Sandel

Michael J. Sandel teaches political philosophy at Harvard University in Cambridge, Massachusetts. He is also the author of The Case against Perfection: Ethics in the Age of Genetic Engineering.

There are serious contradictions in President George W. Bush's embryonic stem cell policy. If he and other pro-lifers believe that embryonic stem cell research is destroying human life—and that embryos are the moral equivalent of a human being—then it follows that embryonic stem cell research is the same as murder. Not only must President Bush ban the practice, but researchers that work with embryonic stem cells and in vitro fertilization clinics that discard excess embryos should be liable for criminal prosecution for murder.

Congress and the president are at odds over a tangled question at the boundary of science, ethics, and religion. President [George W.] Bush has restricted federal funding of embryonic stem cell research, and [in 2006] cast the first veto of his presidency when Congress tried to ease the restriction. . . .

The main arguments are by now familiar. Proponents argue that embryonic stem cell research holds great promise for

understanding and curing diabetes, Parkinson's disease, spinal cord injury, and other debilitating conditions. Opponents argue that the research is unethical, because deriving the stem cells destroys the blastocyst, an unimplanted human embryo at the sixth to eighth day of development. As Bush declared when he vetoed [the 2006] stem cell bill, the federal government should not support "the taking of innocent human life."

The Moral Issue

It is surprising that, despite the extensive public debate—in Congress, during the 2004 and 2006 election campaigns, and on the Sunday morning talk shows—relatively little attention has been paid to the moral issue at the heart of the controversy: Are the opponents of stem cell research correct in their claim that the unimplanted human embryo is already a human being, morally equivalent to a person?

Perhaps this claim has gone unaddressed because stem cell proponents and many in the media consider it obviously false, a faith-based belief that no rational argument could possibly dislodge. If so, they are making a mistake.

It is important to grasp the full force of the claim that the embryo is morally equivalent to a person.

The fact that a moral belief may be rooted in religious conviction neither exempts it from challenge nor puts it beyond the realm of public debate. Ignoring the claim that the blastocyst is a person fails to respect those who oppose embryonic stem cell research on principled moral grounds. It has also led the media to miss glaring contradictions in Bush's stem cell policy, which does not actually live up to the principle it invokes—that destroying an embryo is like killing a child.

Blastocysts Examined

It is important to be clear, first of all, about the embryo from which stem cells are extracted. It is not implanted and growing in a woman's uterus. It is not a fetus. It has no recognizable human features or form. It is, rather, a blastocyst, a cluster of 180 to 200 cells, growing in a petri dish, barely visible to the naked eye. Such blastocysts are either cloned in the lab or created in fertility clinics. . . . Congress would fund stem cell research only on excess blastocysts left over from infertility treatments.

The blastocyst represents such an early stage of embryonic development that the cells it contains have not yet differentiated, or taken on the properties of particular organs or tissues—kidneys, muscles, spinal cord, and so on. This is why the stem cells that are extracted from the blastocyst hold the promise of developing, with proper coaxing in the lab, into any kind of cell the researcher wants to study or repair.

The moral and political controversy arises from the fact that extracting the stem cells destroys the blastocyst. It is important to grasp the full force of the claim that the embryo is morally equivalent to a person, a fully developed human being. For those who hold this view, extracting stem cells from a blastocyst is as morally abhorrent as harvesting organs from a baby to save other people's lives. This is the position of Senator Sam Brownback, Republican of Kansas, a leading advocate of the right-to-life position. In Brownback's view, "a human embryo . . . is a human being just like you and me; and it deserves the same respect that our laws give to us all."

Is a Blastocyst Human?

If Brownback is right, then embryonic stem cell research is immoral because it amounts to killing a person to treat other people's diseases. But is he right? Is there good reason to believe that the blastocyst is a person?

31

Some base this belief on the religious conviction that the soul enters the body at the moment of conception. Others defend it without recourse to religion, by the following line of reasoning:

Human beings are not things. Their lives must not be sacrificed against their will, even for the sake of good ends, like saving other people's lives. The reason human beings must not be treated as things is that they are inviolable. At what point do we acquire this inviolability? The answer cannot depend on the age or developmental stage of a particular human life. Infants are inviolable, and few people would countenance harvesting organs for transplantation even from a fetus. Every human being—each one of us—began life as an embryo. Unless we can point to a definitive moment in the passage from conception to birth that marks the emergence of the human person, we must regard embryos as possessing the same inviolability as fully developed human beings.

Challenging the Belief

This argument can be challenged on a number of grounds. First, it is undeniable that a human embryo is "human life" in the biological sense that it is living rather than dead, and human rather than, say, bovine. But this biological fact does not establish that the blastocyst is a human being, or a person. Any living human cell (a skin cell, for example) is "human life" in the sense of being human rather than bovine and living rather than dead. But no one would consider a skin cell a person, or deem it inviolable. Showing that a blastocyst is a human being, or a person, requires further argument.

Some try to base such an argument on the fact that human beings develop from embryo to fetus to child. Every person was once an embryo, the argument goes, and there is no clear, non-arbitrary line between conception and adulthood that can tell us when personhood begins. Given the lack of

such a line, we should regard the blastocyst as a person, as morally equivalent to a fully developed human being.

If harvesting stem cells from a blastocyst were truly on a par with harvesting organs from a baby, then the morally responsible policy would be to ban it, not merely deny it federal funding.

But this argument is not persuasive. Consider an analogy: although every oak tree was once an acorn, it does not follow that acorns are oak trees, or that I should treat the loss of an acorn eaten by a squirrel in my front yard as the same kind of loss as the death of an oak tree felled by a storm. Despite their developmental continuity, acorns and oak trees differ. So do human embryos and human beings, and in the same way. Just as acorns are potential oaks, human embryos are potential human beings.

The distinction between a potential person and an actual one makes a moral difference. Sentient creatures make claims on us that nonsentient ones do not; beings capable of experience and consciousness make higher claims still. Human life develops by degrees.

Another Reason for Skepticism

A further reason to be skeptical of the notion that blastocysts are persons is to notice that many who invoke it do not embrace its full implications. President Bush is a case in point. In 2001, he announced a policy that restricted federal funding to already existing stem cell lines, so that no taxpayer funds would encourage or support the destruction of embryos. And in 2006, he vetoed a bill that would have funded new embryonic stem cell research, saying that he did not want to support "the taking of innocent human life."

But it is a striking feature of the president's position that, while restricting the funding of embryonic stem cell research,

he has made no effort to ban it. To adapt a slogan from the [Bill] Clinton administration [i.e., "Don't Ask, Don't Tell"], the Bush policy might be summarized as "don't fund, don't ban." But this policy is at odds with the notion that embryos are human beings.

If harvesting stem cells from a blastocyst were truly on a par with harvesting organs from a baby, then the morally responsible policy would be to ban it, not merely deny it federal funding. If some doctors made a practice of killing children to get organs for transplantation, no one would take the position that the infanticide should be ineligible for federal funding but allowed to continue in the private sector. In fact, if we were persuaded that embryonic stem cell research were tantamount to infanticide, we would not only ban it but treat it as a grisly form of murder and subject scientists who performed it to criminal punishment.

Contradiction in Policy

It might be argued, in defense of the president's policy, that Congress would be unlikely to enact an outright ban on embryonic stem cell research. But this does not explain why, if the president really considers embryos to be human beings, he has not at least called for such a ban, nor even called upon scientists to stop doing stem cell research that involves the destruction of embryos. In fact, Bush has cited the fact that "there is no ban on embryonic stem cell research" in touting the virtues of his "balanced approach."

The moral oddness of the Bush "don't fund, don't ban" position confused even his spokesman, Tony Snow. [In 2006], Snow told the White House press corps that the president vetoed the stem cell bill because he considered embryonic stem cell research to be "murder," something the federal government should not support. When the comment drew a flurry of critical press attention, the White House retreated. No, the president did not believe that destroying an embryo was mur-

der. The press secretary retracted his statement, and apologized for having "overstated the president's position."

> *Those who fail to take seriously the belief that embryos are persons ... should ask why the president does not pursue the full implications of the principle he invokes.*

How exactly the spokesman had overstated the president's position is unclear. If embryonic stem cell research does constitute the deliberate taking of innocent human life, it is hard to see how it differs from murder. The chastened press secretary made no attempt to parse the distinction. His errant statement that the president considered embryo destruction to be "murder" simply followed the moral logic of the notion that embryos are human beings. It was a gaffe only because the Bush policy does not follow that logic.

The president's refusal to ban privately-funded embryonic stem cell research is not the only way in which his policies betray the principle that embryos are persons. In the course of treating infertility, American fertility clinics routinely discard thousands of human embryos. The bill before the Senate [in 2007] would fund stem cell research only on these excess embryos, which are already bound for destruction.... Although Bush would ban the use of such embryos in federally funded research, he has not called for legislation to ban the creation and destruction of embryos by fertility clinics.

But if embryos are human beings, to allow fertility clinics to discard them is to countenance, in effect, the widespread creation and destruction of surplus children. Those who believe that a blastocyst is morally equivalent to a baby must believe that the 400,000 excess embryos languishing in freezers in US fertility clinics are like newborns left to die by exposure on a mountainside. But those who view embryos in this way should not only be opposing embryonic stem cell research;

they should also be leading a campaign to shut down what they must regard as rampant infanticide in fertility clinics.

Pro-lifers Must Be Consistent

Some principled right-to-life opponents of stem cell research meet this test of moral consistency. Bush's "don't fund, don't ban" policy does not. Those who fail to take seriously the belief that embryos are persons miss this point. Rather than simply complain that the president's stem cell policy allows religion to trump science, critics should ask why the president does not pursue the full implications of the principle he invokes.

If he does not want to ban embryonic stem cell research, or prosecute stem cell scientists for murder, or ban fertility clinics from creating and discarding excess embryos, this must mean that he does not really consider human embryos as morally equivalent to fully developed human beings after all.

But if he doesn't believe that embryos are persons, then why ban federally funded embryonic stem cell research that holds promise for curing diseases and saving lives?

Adult Stem Cells Are More Valuable than Embryonic Stem Cells

Michael Fumento

Michael Fumento is an associate of the Competitive Enterprise Institute and a senior fellow at the Hudson Institute. He is also the author of BioEvolution: How Biotechnology Is Changing Our World.

The reason that public opinion favors embryonic stem cell research is that people are ignorant of the facts: adult stem cells routinely treat or cure 80 different diseases, while embryonic stem cells are largely untested. The media are responsible for this injustice because they are lazy, intolerant of religious values, and manipulated by the embryonic stem cell research industry. The truth is that adult stem cell research is currently having more real breakthroughs and treating more diseases than embryonic stem cell research.

There's little doubt that opponents of embryonic stem cell (ESC) research have their work cut out for them. Polls repeatedly show large majorities (in the 60–70 percent range) want the federal government to promote and fund the research. Californians backed their opinions with money with 59 percent of those who showed up at the polls voting for last November's [2004] Proposition 71, which will funnel $3 billion of the cash-strapped state's funds into embryonic stem-cell research over the next decade.

But why—on a scientific issue, about which most people know relatively little—does public opinion seem so lopsided?

Why Public Approval?

One explanation is that the polls often feature loaded questions that begin with tales of the medical miracles ESCs will allegedly bring us: cures for Parkinson's, Alzheimer's, diabetes, you name it. They don't even try to find out whether respondents really have any idea of what ESC research is. And as a rule, they don't mention possible alternatives—namely, so-called adult stem cells (ASCs), which are obtained without the ethical conflicts of harvesting human embryos.

But the biggest reason may simply be that the mainstream media are doing a lousy job of informing the public on the state of stem-cell science. By and large, they're telling people all about the potential of ESCs—especially the supposed ability to become any type of cell—without talking about certain little drawbacks, like a tendency for ESCs to be rejected and even to become cancerous.

Perhaps more important, the media aren't telling people how much more advanced ASC research is, or how rapidly it's making breakthroughs. Certainly they're not telling people about it nearly as often as they're hailing the promise of ESCs—and when they do, they tend to undermine the news with pooh-poohing, often-groundless quotes from ESC advocates. (More on that later.)

As a science writer who has covered the topic extensively, I know something about this. I see the media coverage practically every day. On rare occasions I'll find blatant falsehoods: Last August [2004], for example, influential *New York Times* science writer Gina Kolata told readers "so far, no one has succeeded" in getting adult stem cells to treat diseases. That statement either reveals startling ignorance or is an outright lie: Adult stem cells routinely treat or cure more than

80 different diseases, while no ESC research is anywhere near becoming a human clinical trial.

Usually, though, I see something less blatant, but perhaps more harmful: a subtle but persistent bias in reporters' choice of subject matter, interview subjects and quotes, all skewing the reader toward embryonic stem cells and away from any alternatives.

Nor am I the only one who's noticed.

I talked to a number of stem-cell researchers and the only journalist willing to be interviewed for this story and found a consensus that there's a strong media bias. What interested me most, though, were their thoughts on how and why that bias comes into play—and the role of factors like attitudes toward religion, manipulation by the pro-ESC lobby, and just plain ignorance and laziness.

As [pro–embryonic stem cell] reporters picture themselves standing for the cause of reason against the forces of dogma, they also don't realize that the ESC research vocabulary ... reflects a dogma all its own.

Media Biases

Many pro-lifers suspect that the media's pro-ESC bias has to do with their politics on issues like abortion and euthanasia. There may be something to that, but it's hard to pinpoint. The only major example is a 2001 *Newsweek* column by Anna Quindlen, who spoke warmly of the prospect that fetal-tissue and ESC treatments could soften public opposition toward abortion, bringing "a certain long-overdue relativism to discussions of abortion across the board."

More likely what's going on involves reporters' attitudes toward religion—or more precisely, religion in science and public-policy debates. In their minds, ESC backers have a purely scientific motivation while ASC backers have a religious

one. Many journalists may see themselves as defending science against religion: They may have missed Galileo's trial, but by golly they're here for this one. (That attitude is sometimes seen most clearly outside the mainstream media. In the liberal magazine *The American Prospect*, for example, Chris Mooney wrote a recent piece sneering at "the Christian right's new 'science.'")

There's a great irony here, however. As these reporters picture themselves standing for the cause of reason against the forces of dogma, they also don't realize that the ESC research vocabulary—so filled with "mays" and "coulds" and "one days," promising a miraculous future somewhere down the road—reflects a dogma all its own.

Consider Harvard's Douglas Melton, a diabetes researcher better known for attacking successful ASC efforts than making any real progress on his own with ESCs. He's one of the most-quoted stem-cell experts in the country, and was named Policy Leader of the Year for 2004 by the politically correct *Scientific American* for having "advocated and enabled more extensive studies of embryonic stem cells."

But what, precisely, has Melton accomplished toward curing diabetes with ESCs? When interviewed by *The Wall Street Journal* [in 2004], the most he could say was "We are convinced we can do it. We just don't know how."

That's not science; that's faith. But it's not a religious faith, and so reporters don't see it for what it is.

Ignorance and Sloth

In asking why ESCs get better press, it's important to bear in mind that while investigative journalism may not be dead, it's certainly on life support.

Most reporters get their information the same way you do—from other reporters. To the extent they use a primary source, such as an interview subject, they get their names from other reporters as well. You've heard the term "famous

for being famous," but likewise the world is full of people who are experts for no other reason that at some point somebody in the media anointed them one.

"They pick a couple of favorites and take a quote and that's it," complains Dr. David Prentice. Prentice is a biologist and former ASC researcher who's now a senior fellow for life sciences at the Family Research Council [FRC] in Washington, D.C. "Most reporters just want a sound bite—[either] a controversial sound bite or one that backs up their preconceived notion. For some reason, they don't want to report."

Reporters are busy and deadline-oriented, and as much as they complain of being "flacked" by PR [public relations] departments, their choice of stories, of angles and expert quotes is often determined by which side hits them first with an e-mail or phone call.

There's no question that the ESC lobby has the upper hand here. It's organized and it's wealthy: In the case of California's Proposition 71, supporters outspent opponents by 62-1. Because the text of the Proposition runs to 9,000 words, voters didn't read it; advertising and media coverage made all the difference.

The very fact that the science isn't on their side dictates that the ESC lobby must do something to make up for it—so they work the press, to their benefit. ASC researchers feel much less pressure, often believing success is the best PR—so they neglect the press, to their detriment.

Case in point: Ira Black, a neurologist at the Robert Wood Johnson Medical School, is one of the most important ASC researchers in the country, the author or co-author of more than 200 peer-reviewed studies. He's also head of one of four labs that has published results showing the ability to convert ASCs into all three "germ layers" formed during early embryonic development. (One gives rise to connective tissues, muscles, and the circulatory system. One leads to development

of the skin and the nervous system. The last gives rise to the gastrointestinal tract, respiratory tract, and endocrine glands.)

The importance of such findings can't be overstated, since the only advantage ESCs ever appeared to have over ASCs was the ability to become all cell types. With that gone, the excuse for ESC research vanishes.

Yet judging by the Nexis media database, Black gets about a fourth of the publicity of the aforementioned ESC enthusiast Douglas Melton.

Black says he believes the media are biased toward ESCs, and the main reason is simple ignorance. "We [scientists] have to do a better job educating altogether," he says. "We're not doing the best job we can do." Yet when asked if his department had so much as put out press releases, he said no. "It's not my job; I'm a scientist and a physician."

More Media Savvy

That attitude may be understandable, but it's not good enough, according to Boston cardiologist Douglas Losordo—because it doesn't address "the reality of our [mass media] culture."

Losordo heads another lab that converted marrow cells into those of all three major categories. He's frustrated that even "our legislators don't even know about" what's being done with ASCs, he says. "Part of our job as scientists is to publish to colleagues, but part of it is also to help educate the public."

> ESC [embryonic stem cell] advocates, . . . are not only enthusiastic promoters of their product, they have no hesitation about trashing the competition.

If a lot of adult stem-cell researchers aren't exactly media-savvy evangelists for their cause, it's important to recognize some of the reasons their voices are muted.

ASC researchers fear having their funds cut off by the National Institutes of Health [NIH], which—despite the limitations laid down by President [George W.] Bush—is seen as overwhelmingly biased toward ESC research. A search of the NIH grant database from 2001 to the present, using the term "embryonic stem cell," brings up a list of 750 grants. For ASCs the list is a mere 140, with an additional 139 for umbilical-cord stem cells.

ASC researchers also fear having their papers turned down by the major publications. The two most prestigious science journals in the world, *Science* and *Nature*, are overwhelmingly pro-ESC research, but do run some papers presenting the benefits of ASCs. So ASC researchers figure they have a chance of getting published—if they pay homage to the editors' enthusiasm for embryonic stem cells.

Between concerns over money and publication, you can see why researchers aren't eager to make enemies by criticizing the potential of embryonic stem cells. (No one wants to be heard bashing the boss's fair-haired boy.) Sometimes ASC researchers let their true beliefs slip: I'll hear them say things like "adult stem-cell research is what's on the move; embryonic stem cells are going to fade in the rearview mirror." Yet they'll quickly catch themselves and, in the same breath, insist that, "of course, it's important to keep researching embryonic stem cells."

Trashing the Competition

ESC advocates, by contrast, are not only enthusiastic promoters of their product, they have no hesitation about trashing the competition.

While ASC researchers like Black or Losordo may get calls from reporters if they've just published an exciting new discovery, those same reporters (to "add balance") make sure they give a counter-quote from ESC advocates like Harvard's

Melton, or Stanford's Irving Weissman. Those men will often say things that are, simply, ludicrous—and they get away with it.

In a recent *Washington Monthly* piece by Chris Mooney, for example, Weissman claimed there is "no independently verified evidence today" that a non-embryonic stem cell of one type "can turn into another [type of] tissue at all." Sure, that claim is contradicted by countless published, peer-reviewed papers to the contrary, all available at the push of a few keys at the free Internet database *PubMed*. (One was even co-authored by Weissman.) But reporters feel a quote from a prominent credentialed ESC booster gets them off the hook from having to do that simple search.

"Whether there's any evidence to the contrary or not, reporters don't bother to check," says the FRC's Prentice.

Yet it's even worse than that. If Melton or Weissman thought reporters would do additional research, they wouldn't make such comments. They count on journalists' ignorance and laziness—and they get it.

"It is clear that the media devote more attention to ESCs than ASCs," says the *National Journal*'s Neil Munro. "The question is, why editors don't assign more knowledgeable reporters. It's up to editors to train and assign reporters and assign only those knowledgeable enough to challenge claims."

Few Reporters Aware of Facts

Munro is one of the few media people who do just that. His articles on stem-cell politics are not only brilliant but consistently contain more investigative reporting than a week's worth of the *New York Times*—or a year of *USA Today*. For example, a few years ago he dug up a very relevant fact: Some of the top ESC advocates have big money in what they're promoting. Weissman has co-founded several stem-cell companies through which he's made millions of dollars (Including Stem Cells, Inc.), and Melton co-founded a couple as well (most notably Curis, Inc.).

In a November 2002 article, Munro lambasted the media for almost never informing "readers that these supposedly disinterested scientists have great financial stakes in the debate." That hasn't changed. Indeed, a Nexis search this March [2005] found over 600 mentions of Weissman and stem cells, but only 23 that included his affiliation with Stem Cells, Inc.; the rest merely associated him with Stanford. There were 344 mentions of Melton and stem cells mentioning his Harvard connection; just two mentioned Curis (and one of those was written by Munro).

"Reporters don't treat scientists as entrepreneurs," says Munro, "and I suspect it has something to do with scientists advertising their affiliation with universities rather than traditional corporations," he says.

ASC researchers . . . are almost always practicing physicians. They watch people suffer; they watch them die. They want to help them and to do so as soon as possible.

Ultimately it all becomes one big vicious circle, with the facts left out. The result, essentially, is an urban legend— begun by a few, maintained by many. And urban legends die hard.

But surely there are reporters who understand stem cells enough and write for big enough publications that they know about the urban legends, know how to use *PubMed* and know there are more than two stem-cell experts in the entire country. There are: the designated science writers. But they may be worst of all, says Munro.

Readers want to hear what science will do for them or their loved ones, but, "What science reporters are interested in is the advancement of science, not the end results," says Munro. "Part of the reason ASCs don't get attention is that science reporters don't think they're interesting."

In this, suggests Munro, they're akin to ESC researchers themselves. Not all of them are looking to become millionaires by selling patents. But they've chosen Petri dishes over patients. They'll talk about curing diseases, because they know that's what the public wants to hear. But they're no more focused on people than is an astronomer or physicist. All too often, Munro says, "it has nothing to do with curing people or treating diseases."

ASC Researchers Care About People

Which brings out yet another irony. Embryonic stem-cell backers often charge their critics with caring for abstract religious doctrine, not for suffering people. Yet that description arguably may be best suited to many if not most of the ESC advocates themselves. ASC researchers, on the other hand, are almost always practicing physicians. They watch people suffer; they watch them die. They want to help them and to do so as soon as possible.

Will Ambler would agree. He lost the use of his legs 12 years ago at age 24 and is determined to one day—soon—trash his wheelchair with the help of ASCs. Ambler is a focused young man who has started a philanthropy to raise funds for spinal regeneration on humans using ASCs. And he's not impressed with the embryonic stem-cell lobby.

"They've done a good job of misleading people into thinking it will produce a panacea for all human maladies," he says. "And so the public has demanded ESC work because they're misled." Meanwhile, he says, "maybe billions of dollars and millions of lives will be wasted."

That's something the public has a right to know.

Adult Stem Cells Are Not More Valuable than Embryonic Stem Cells

Steven Edwards

Steven Edwards is a contributor to Wired *magazine.*

The use of adult stem cell treatment carries a serious risk. Recent statistics show that more than five thousand people have died as a result of bone marrow transplants and graft-versus-host disease. These are shocking numbers because pro-life forces are trying to convince the public that the use of adult stem cells is safer than embryonic stem cells. These appalling statistics belie that assertion. Society should keep politics out of the issue and provide ample funding to scientists to pursue both adult and embryonic stem cell research.

A dult stem cells kill.

They're mass murderers, in fact. In only five years between 2000 and 2004, adult stem cells used in some 25,000 bone marrow transplant treatments have been complicit in at least 3,629 American deaths, 624 of which involved children under the age of 18, according to the National Center for Health Statistics. If the trend continues, adult stem cells will claim their 5,000th victim since 2000 [in 2007].

Now the shocking part: To the best of my knowledge, these numbers are appearing for the first time publicly in this

article. The data is scattered among some 12 million lines of text at the National Bureau of Economic Research website. No easily accessible summary report is available. I wrote a Perl [computer programming language] script to extract the information.

"I've never heard that statistic before," says John Hlinko, founder of the pro-embryonic-stem-cell lobbying group Stem-Pac.

Arguments that adult stem cells are better than embryonic stem cells are in full swing [in April 2007] as legislators debate the Stem Cell Research Enhancement Act (SB5). This politically explosive bill would overturn federal stem cell restrictions, allowing researchers to use embryos from fertility clinics that would otherwise be discarded. The senate is scheduled to vote on the bill Thursday [April 12, 2007], and conservatives have rallied opposition. Even if it passes, a veto is expected.

Stem cells of both varieties show enormous promise for seemingly miraculous medical treatments, from reversing the effects of Alzheimer's disease to repairing a damaged spinal cord. But, eager to keep embryonic stem cells out of the labs, some conservatives insist adult stem cells are so promising that embryonic stem cells need not be considered at all.

Ignoring the Dangers

They make three common claims about adult stem cells: They already work as therapies, while embryonic stem cells are still experimental; they are derived without killing embryos; and—last but not least—they are safe compared to embryonic stem cells, which are known to cause tumors.

In fact, the risks of graft versus host disease, or GVHD, following bone marrow transplants are well documented by the National Cancer Institute. Early reports of GVHD, then known as "runt disease," were enough of a concern to merit mention in a 1960 Nobel Lecture, so the risks have been known for more than 40 years.

Complications of acute GVHD arise from attacks against the skin, liver and intestines. They range from mild—skin rash, nausea and cramping—to severe: blisters, bloody diarrhea and death. Chronic GVHD complications include attacks on the aforementioned organs, as well as any other organ.

Let's give scientists ample funding to solve potential complications and let the science lead the way.

Nevertheless, organizations including the Family Research Council, The Center for Bioethics and Human Dignity, World-NetDaily and Do No Harm all recite the same argument: Therapies derived from embryonic stem cells will form tumors, therefore the risks are too great to justify spending the public's money to study them. Instead, they say, adult stem cells—taken from bone marrow, blood, hair follicles and various other locations without harming the human body—are a better use of taxpayer money.

That embryonic stem cell supporters haven't tallied the numbers is astonishing, given the aggressive tactics of those who attack embryonic stem cell research. David Prentice, senior fellow for life sciences at the Family Research Council, and Sen. Dave Weldon (R-Florida) have both publicly claimed that adult stem cells are inherently safe.

Adult Stem Cells a Risk

Bob Lanza, vice president of research and scientific development at Advanced Cell Technology, said highlighting the risks of adult versus embryonic stem cells misses the point.

Embryonic stem cell researchers "are actually at a disadvantage because the majority of scientists say we should not be pitting adult versus embryonic stem cells," Lanza said. "We need to pursue all these avenues and in the end there are going to be literally hundreds of diseases that could be treated with stem cells, and we don't know which kind will be best for which diseases."

Maybe ignoring the risks of adult stem cells is an honest mistake by adult stem cell boosters. A less charitable explanation is that they knowingly mislead the public about the safety of adult stem cells, glossing over GVHD deaths in their desire to discredit embryonic stem cell research.

Granted, the risk of GVHD is one a leukemia patient is usually willing to take. Similarly, people like me who are waiting for cures might be willing to take certain risks associated with embryonic stem cell therapies.

In the meantime, let's at least have an honest debate. Let's give scientists ample funding to solve potential complications and let the science lead the way.

The Stem Cell Debate Is Really About Funding

Michael D. Tanner

Michael D. Tanner is the director of health and welfare studies at the Cato Institute, a libertarian research organization.

The controversy about stem cell research is entirely about funding and whether the government should be involved. Both sides of the debate are guilty of injecting hyperbole and politics into the discussion. Since government will never be able to separate politics from the issues, we need to turn over funding for stem cell research to private investors and get the government out of it.

Ron Reagan addressed the Democratic National Convention [on July 27, 2004], calling on the federal government to support fetal stem cell research. His plea was heartfelt and eloquent, but ultimately missed the point.

First, this is not a debate about whether stem cell research should be legal. It is, and no one in Congress or the [George W.] Bush administration has proposed banning it. In fact, there are at least nine private stem cell research centers across the country. The largest, at Harvard University, employs more than 100 researchers and recently unveiled 17 new stem cell lines.

Michael D. Tanner, "Don't Politicize Stem Cell Research," *Investor's Business Daily*, July 29, 2004. www.cato.org. Copyright © Investor's Business Daily, Inc. 2000–2006. All rights reserved. Reproduced by permission.

No, this is really a fight about money, about whether the federal government should fund the research. And, as such, it is a perfect example of how science becomes politicized when government money is involved.

The vast majority of medical and scientific breakthroughs in this country's history have been accomplished by the private sector. There's no reason for stem cell research to be any different.

For example, all the political rhetoric may have led people to believe that stem cell research is on the verge of producing a cure for Alzheimer's disease. In reality, stem cell research has produced far more promising results in areas such as Parkinson's disease, muscular dystrophy and spinal injuries. But researchers and other supporters of government funding have attractive advocates in Ron Reagan and his mother, Nancy. If the Reagans care about Alzheimer's research, that's what the media will pay attention to, never mind the science.

This has long been the case with government health care spending. Find a "mediagenic" spokesperson and get him on television and you can get your disease funded. Thus we see an endless stream of television and movie stars trooping to Capitol Hill to testify about scientific and medical issues that they know nothing about.

Both Sides Disingenuous

Opponents of stem cell research are just as disingenuous. Every study of adult stem cells is hailed as a miraculous breakthrough, though most scientists believe that fetal stem cells hold far more promise. Opponents have downplayed or ignored studies that go against their views. Even as Ron Reagan was addressing the Democratic convention, the Family Research Council was issuing a press release highlighting "the

failures of embryonic stem cell research." Theirs is ultimately a moral position but they insist on portraying it as a scientific one.

Both sides in this debate have the best of motives. Supporters of fetal stem cell research see it as saving lives and curing horrible diseases. Opponents object to having their tax dollars used for practices that they believe are morally offensive. In the process, both sides end up distorting science.

By its very nature, government politicizes everything it touches. Science is no exception. Stem cell research needs neither government money nor politics. It is better to get the government out and let the private sector continue its good work. Those people calling for increased funding could take out their checkbooks and support it. Those who oppose embryonic stem cell research would not be forced to pay for it.

The vast majority of medical and scientific breakthroughs in this country's history have been accomplished by the private sector. There's no reason for stem cell research to be any different. Let's end the political debate, and get back to scientific research.

8

Embryonic Stem Cell Research Should Be Federally Funded

Jeffrey M. Drazen

Jeffrey M. Drazen is a professor in the Department of Environmental Health at the Harvard University School of Public Health. He is also editor in chief of the New England Journal of Medicine.

Denying federal funding for cutting-edge embryonic stem cell research will mean that we will lose ground to other countries currently putting stem cells to the test. Stem cell technology will be developed abroad, and someday U.S. citizens may be forced to leave the country to benefit from therapeutic technology. We must nurture scientific study, particularly in an area as promising as embryonic stem cell research.

In the debate between those who support federal funding for embryonic stem-cell research and those who do not, a critical point has been overlooked. Research using this technology is strongly supported in a number of countries, including Australia, Israel, the Czech Republic, Singapore, Korea, and the United Kingdom. Others in the world appreciate the potential of this technology. If we continue to prevent federal funds from being used to support this research in the United States, the ability of our biomedical scientists to compete with other research teams throughout the world will be under-

Jeffrey M. Drazen, "Embryonic Stem-Cell Research: The Case for Federal Funding," *The New England Journal of Medicine*, vol. 351, October 21, 2004, pp. 1789–1790. http://content.nejm.org. Copyright © 2004 Massachusetts Medical Society. All rights reserved. Reproduced by permission.

mined. No matter how hard we try, we cannot legislate an end to a process of discovery that many in this country and elsewhere in the world consider ethically justifiable. The work will go on—but outside the United States.

The example of a single disease, diabetes, suggests the range of possibilities. Suppose that next week a group announced that it had successfully performed experiments showing that genetically identical pancreatic beta cells could be grown in tissue culture with use of a donor nucleus from a patient and human embryonic stem cells. If our working community of biomedical scientists had experience with this technology, it would probably take three to six months for the findings to be replicated; without the needed laboratory know-how, as a result of our current federal policy of permitting research with only a limited number of preexisting embryonic stem-cell lines, these experiments could take years to complete, and replication would be likely to happen outside the United States.

[Without federal research funding] our children and grandchildren may need to leave the United States to benefit from treatments other nations are currently developing.

The next critical step would be to show that the pancreatic beta cells could be expanded ex vivo [in the laboratory] to achieve adequate numbers for transplantation and injection into patients with diabetes, where they would "cure" the patients' diabetes. For the data to be convincing, small trials would need to show that the cells functioned as desired for 6 to 12 months in a small number of patients. Again, for this research to be successful, the physicians and scientists who could create and expand the cell lines would need to be trained and ready to participate. Without an experienced workforce,

years could be added to the time required. More than likely, such experiments would have to be conducted outside the United States.

Next, a major clinical trial would need to be mounted. The technology to create the cells for transplantation would have to be expanded to many centers, quality-control measures would need to be put in place, patients recruited, beta-cell lines created, cells injected, and patients followed for at least 30 months. Early research would probably use surrogate end points, such as glycosylated hemoglobin levels; studies with adequate power to detect differences in clinical end points, such as the development of renal failure or vascular events, would take much longer. As a conservative estimate, if the fundamental breakthrough at the laboratory level occurred next week, it would be more than five years before there was a stem-cell–based cure for diabetes. Without federal funding for stem-cell research, a prerequisite to the availability of a well-prepared research workforce, these experiments would probably be conducted outside the United States.

Although five years may seem like a long time, on the scale of therapeutic development it is relatively short. If we fail to bring the necessary research technology into the mainstream now, our children and grandchildren may need to leave the United States to benefit from treatments other nations are currently developing. Our research scientists must be able to adopt and use embryonic stem-cell technology as they pursue its use in the treatment of many degenerative diseases. Such research has promise, but it must be nurtured to flourish.

We hope that the advances resulting from stem-cell technology will bring new tools to medical care. In the hypothetical example described above, progress in research would be reported at each step. As journal editors, we undertake to review dispassionately any work on stem cells that is submitted to us. We pledge to report true advances. But for us to do so,

the journey must be started. As each significant step brings us closer to the goal, we will be there to report the progress; it would be nice if some of this progress could be made within the United States.

9

Embryonic Stem Cell Research May Not Need Federal Funding

Ronald Bailey

Ronald Bailey is the science and technology correspondent for Reason *magazine and Reason.com. He is the author of* Liberation Biology: The Moral and Scientific Case for the Biotech Revolution.

President George W. Bush's limitation of federal spending on embryonic stem cell research has resulted in an increasing number of state initiatives. States such as California have passed initiatives that will fund stem cell research in their states, thereby attracting investment in biotechnology. With other states considering their own funding initiatives, federal funding may not be necessary.

In August 2001, President George [W.] Bush limited federal spending on human embryonic stem-cell research to stem-cell lines derived before that date. President Bush said that he was restricting federal support for research to those lines because he did not want to "encourage further destruction of human embryos that have at least the potential for life." So far only 22 stem-cell lines qualify for federal funding of human embryonic stem-cell research, and the National Institutes of Health provided only $24.3 million [in 2004] for such research. It's impossible to tell what the level of federal funding

for such research would be now in the absence of the administration's restrictions, because it is impossible to know how many good solid research proposals those restrictions have deterred from even being submitted.

State Initiatives

However, these federal funding restrictions have provoked an outpouring of state initiatives for research funding for stem-cell research. So far [as of August 2005] four states have put taxpayer dollars behind human embryonic stem-cell research. The 800 pound gorilla in the stem cell funding arena is California. Last November [2004], California voters passed a $3 billion initiative that created the new California Institute of Regenerative Medicine that aims to fund stem-cell research at $300 million annually for the next ten years. That is more than 12 times higher than current federal funding. California will not only be outspending the U.S. federal government; it will be trouncing whole countries on stem-cell research funding. For example, the United Kingdom has plans to spend $175 million per year on stem-cell research. In 2002, the Australian government awarded the Australia Stem Cell Centre with $43.55 million over four years. And the research of South Korean scientists who have recently been making breakthroughs in cloning human embryonic stem cells has been supported by about $11 million in government grants.

The other three states that have ponied up for stem-cell research are New Jersey, Connecticut, and Illinois. New Jersey has allocated $150 million to construct a new stem-cell research center, and Governor Richard Codey is proposing a November 2006 referendum to ask voters to authorize $230 million to fund the research. Connecticut has passed legislation authorizing $100 million in spending on both adult and embryonic stem-cell research over the next 10 years. In Illinois, Governor Rod Blagojevich moved $10 million of state public health research funding to establish a new stem-cell re-

search institute called the Illinois Regenerative Medicine Institute. This was in lieu of a much more ambitious plan by state Comptroller Dan Hynes, who proposed a $1 billion referendum to create an Illinois Regenerative Medicine Institute that would have dispensed $100 million a year in research grants and loans over the next 10 years. The proposal would have been funded by a 6 percent tax on face-lifts, Botox injections and other cosmetic procedures.

Given all of [the state and private] sources of funding for stem-cell research, it's a real question whether or not researchers need the Feds.

Other States

Many other states are mulling over various proposals to fund stem-cell research. In Massachusetts, legislators are expected to introduce a bill proposing that the state spend $100 million on stem-cell research. In North Carolina, a bill proposing to use $10 million from the state's tobacco settlement proceeds to fund stem-cell research has been introduced in the state legislature. Even in the president's home state, the Texas House of Representatives approved selling $41.1 million in bonds to build a stem-cell research facility at the University of Texas Health Science Center at Houston. (Gov. Rick Perry says that he is against spending taxpayer money on research that ends human life.) In March [2005], legislation was introduced in the New York State Assembly to create the New York State Institute for stem-cell research and Regenerative Medicine with annual funding of $100 million. The Maryland House of Representatives approved a bill allocating $23 million to a stem-cell research fund—the bill died in the state Senate. A bill creating the Pennsylvania Stem-Cell Research Council that would disburse the research funding created through a $500 million

bond initiative paid for by a 2 percent tax on medical devices and diagnostic equipment has been introduced in the Pennsylvania State House.

Private Funding Growing

Setting aside commercial efforts like those of the Geron Corporation, private funding for academic stem-cell research is also rising. For example, the Starr Foundation is providing $50 million over three years for human embryonic stem-cell research at three New York City medical institutions, including the Sloan-Kettering Memorial Cancer Center. The Harvard University Stem Cell Institute is seeking $100 million in private funding. The University of California, Los Angeles announced the establishment of its Institute for Stem Cell Biology and Medicine with $20 million in funding over the next 5 years. Stanford University announced the creation of $120 million Institute for Cancer/Stem Cell Biology and Medicine in 2002. Former Intel CEO Andy Grove gave the University of California in San Francisco a matching grant of $5 million to start its Developmental and Stem Cell Biology Program. In 2001, an anonymous donor gave Johns Hopkins University in Baltimore a $58.5 million gift to launch an Institute for Cell Engineering. The University of Minnesota has set up a Stem Cell Institute with a $15 million capital grant. In 2004, a grateful patient pledged $25 million over the next ten years to finance stem-cell research at the University of Texas Health Science Center in Houston.

Given all of these sources of funding for stem-cell research, it's a real question whether or not researchers need the Feds at this point. And one more deliciously ironic thought: It's just possible that, by imposing his funding restrictions and spurring so many independent initiatives, President Bush has actually caused the creation of more embryonic stem cell lines than would have been produced with federal funding.

Embryonic Stem Cell Research Should Be Privately Funded

Sigrid Fry-Revere

Sigrid Fry-Revere is director of bioethics studies at the Cato Institute, a libertarian research organization.

Government funding of stem cell research is inevitably politicized and ends up tainting and stalling scientific progress. Private funding, however, is devoid of political considerations and can move stem cell research forward.

Stem cell research has the potential to cure more diseases than any other medical advance in recent memory—and perhaps in history altogether. On face, the impulse to fund such research federally is admirable, but as President [George W.] Bush and the Democratic Congress duke it out, we see why government funding has historically done more to stall than advance controversial medical research.

Two stem cell funding bills passed the Senate [in April 2007] . . . : one, sponsored by Democrats, that would fund research on any embryo destined to be discarded, and another, introduced by Republicans, that does little to further research because it only allows funding for research that won't harm embryos.

It's better to allow private interests to fund the most promising research than to allow the party in power to make medical and scientific decisions for all. In 2005, California passed

Proposition 71, committing $3 billion in state funding to stem cell research, and since then, not a cent of that money has been spent. Private donations and loans—including some from the state's general fund—are making moderate progress on stem cells, but the money authorized by Prop. 71 remains tied up in lawsuits filed by those who oppose the research on moral grounds.

It'll be at least another year before California can issue the bonds to raise the funding, let alone distribute it. And these being bonds, they'll saddle California taxpayers with an additional $3 billion in interest payments over the next 30 years.

Private Funding Works

By contrast, in Missouri, voters [in 2006] passed a constitutional amendment protecting the right to pursue all forms of stem cell research allowed under federal law—but not funding it. This ensured that the state kept the door open for private laboratories like the Stowers Institute for Medical Research, which employs an international team of researchers and $2 billion in private endowments. For years, Stowers has been doing extraordinary research on adult stem cells, and the amendment will see to it that the progress continues as the lab expands into embryonic stem cell research in the future. And since it's privately funded, there'll be no bond issues, no debts, no interest to pay, and no taxpayer liability.

The great advantage of private funding is that it allows research to proceed even—especially—when it is politically touchy.

Stowers has shown tremendous success in adult stem cell research. [In early 2007], they documented the development of cancer stem cells. And they discovered the mechanism by which certain stem cells regenerate themselves—a process essential to therapies that may one day heal damaged organ tis-

sue. They are working now to expand current research programs to include embryonic stem cell research.

Medical research has never ground to a halt when government has declined to support it. The *Journal of the American Medical Association* reported [in] September [2006] that between 1994 and 2003, the U.S. nearly tripled spending on biomedical research, and in any year where federal funding decreased, private funding increased to make up for the difference. The private sector can easily compensate for fluctuations in government spending, and more importantly, can move forward without any federal funding at all.

Advantages of Private Funding

The great advantage of private funding is that it allows research to proceed even—especially—when it is politically touchy. When the federal government refused to fund in-vitro fertilization [IVF] research in the mid-1970s, critics cried that the U.S. would fall behind, that there would be a brain drain, and that infertile couples would suffer. None of these dire predictions came true. Instead, the research proceeded privately and today reproductive technologies—IVF and related technologies for humans and animals—represent a $16 billion a year industry in the U.S. alone.

So not surprisingly, when President Bush exercised the first and only veto of his presidency to stop federal funding for embryonic stem cell research in 2006, private interests donated millions upon millions of dollars to continue embryonic stem cell research without federal assistance.

Now, when private laboratories are already in motion, the Senate is sending over to the House a ham-handed bill that would threaten everything our scientists are already accomplishing. The lure of federal funding would pervert existing incentives, prompting laboratories to abandon productive but politically sensitive research for politically safe but less promising work.

Even Michael J. Fox's own Foundation for Parkinson's Research seems to have given up on government action. [In March 2007], Fox's foundation made a significant contribution to ReNeuron, a private stem cell research laboratory. The actual dollar amount of the donation remains undisclosed, but ReNeuron officials claim that it is large enough to cover their operating costs and accelerate their research efforts for at least the next year.

No doubt it's hard for Senators to accept that progress can happen without them, but if they'd really like to see stem cells do wonders, they should leave the funding to the private sector, and the research decisions to the researchers. Let the labs get on with their work: discovering the cures for what ails us.

Biotechnology Can Find an Ethical Solution to the Stem Cell Debate

Markus Grompe and Robert P. George

Markus Grompe is a professor of genetics at Oregon Health and Science University, director of the Oregon Stem Cell Center, and a member of the International Society for Stem Cell Research. Robert P. George serves on the President's Council on Bioethics and is a professor at Princeton University.

Biotechnology should focus on stem cell research that does not require the destruction or harming of living human embryos. This would sidestep the ethical and moral debate over embryonic stem cell research. There are a few new technologies being developed that show real promise toward this end, and government should fund them.

It is clear that, at least until 2009, there will be no federal money for research involving stem cells derived from embryos destroyed after Aug. 9, 2001. Americans are divided as to whether this is good or bad, but it is the one thing about which there is now no debate.

President Bush's [2006] veto need not mean that new embryonic or embryonic-type stem-cell lines eligible for federal funding cannot be developed, however. The President's Council on Bioethics, in a recent White Paper, identified several

Markus Grompe and Robert P. George, "Creative Science Will Resolve Stem-Cell Issues," *Wall Street Journal*, June 20, 2005, p. A-14. Copyright © 2005 Dow Jones & Company, Inc. All rights reserved. Reprinted with permission of *The Wall Street Journal*.

possible methods for producing such lines that do not require the destruction or harming of living human embryos. There is good scientific reason to believe that this can be done using existing biotechnologies. These possibilities point the way towards a resolution of our nation's divisive debate over embryonic stem-cell harvesting—one that can be embraced in good conscience by people on both sides of the ethical divide.

Revisiting the Debate

What is fascinating about embryonic stem cells, and makes many people believe that someday they will have important therapeutic value (though they have not demonstrated such value as yet), is their "pluripotency"—their capacity to form any and every type of human body cell. But a stem cell (even an embryonic stem cell) is not an embryo; it is not "totipotent"—that is, capable of developing to the next stage of maturity as a new individual of the species. Unlike an embryo, a stem cell is not a complete organism in the beginning stages of its natural development. It is merely part of the larger organism, like any other body cell.

The ethical problem arises because human pluripotent stem cells are obtained today by destroying living human embryos. The solution, if technically feasible, is to produce human pluripotent stem cells directly, that is, without first creating an embryo which must be destroyed or damaged in the process of harvesting stem cells.

OAR Technology

One promising option is called oocyte assisted reprogramming (OAR). This is a variation of a broader concept known as altered nuclear transfer. It combines basic cloning technology with what is known as epigenetic reprogramming.

In cloning, the nucleus of a somatic cell (such as a skin cell) is transferred to an egg cell whose nucleus has been removed. An electrical stimulus is administered in a way that, if

all goes as planned, triggers the development of a new and distinct organism, an embryo, that is virtually identical in its genetic constitution to the organism from which the somatic cell was taken. In OAR, however, the somatic cell nucleus or the egg cytoplasm or both would first be altered before the nucleus is transferred. The modifications would change the expression of certain "master genes"—transcription factors that control expression of many other genes by switching them on or off.

Creative science can help us find a way forward and thus put pluripotent stem-cell research on a footing that all citizens can enthusiastically support.

These genetic alterations would permit the egg to reprogram the somatic cell nucleus directly to a pluripotent, but not a totipotent (i.e., embryonic) state. The altered expression of the powerful control gene would ensure that the characteristics of the newly produced cell are immediately different from, and incompatible with, those of an embryo. For optimal reprogramming, master genes known to control the pluripotency of embryonic stem cells would be used, for example the transcription factor known as "nanog." Thus, we would reasonably expect to obtain precisely the type of stem cells desired by advocates of embryonic stem-cell research, without ever creating or killing embryos.

This method of obtaining human pluripotent stem cells would not only be morally unimpeachable (assuming nothing unethical is done in obtaining somatic cells or oocytes used in the process), it would have other important advantages over using so-called spare embryos left over from in vitro fertilization [IVF] efforts. Unlike stem cells from IVF embryos, scientists could control the genetic structure of OAR-produced stem cells. Their genetic constitution would be virtually identical to that of the donor, thus helping to overcome the problem of immune rejection.

Skirting the Ethical Impasse

Our proposal is not the only possible way for pluripotent stem-cell science to work around the ethical impasse. Progress has recently been reported on another strategy similar to OAR, but using embryonic stem cells, rather than eggs, for reprogramming adult cells to the pluripotent state. Like OAR, further research is needed to confirm that this "cell fusion" strategy will work. If it does, the required embryonic cells could be taken from lines created prior to Aug. 9, 2001, making this research eligible for federal funding.

When he announced his intention of vetoing the embryonic stem-cell bill, President Bush noted that researchers are exploring "different ethical ways of getting the same kind of cells now taken from embryos without violating human life or dignity." He added: "With the right policies and the right techniques, we can pursue scientific progress while still fulfilling our moral duties." The country will likely remain divided about the ethics of research using human embryos. But we believe that creative science can help us find a way forward and thus put pluripotent stem-cell research on a footing that all citizens can enthusiastically support. That would be a great day for science, for morality, and for our nation.

The Stem Cell Debate Is Over

Ryan T. Anderson

Ryan T. Anderson is the assistant director of the Program in Bio-ethics at the Witherspoon Institute of Princeton, New Jersey, and an assistant editor at First Things: The Journal of Religion, Culture, and Public Life.

With new advancements in stem cell research, scientists are reporting that they can produce pluripotent human stem cells without using embryos, eggs, or human cloning. Essentially, this puts an end to the stem cell debate. Now scientists can pursue stem cell research without dealing with the ethical, moral, and political issues that hindered them for years.

The stem cell wars are over. Leading scientists are telling us that they can pursue the most promising stem cell research without using—much less killing—human embryos. This breakthrough enables researchers to create human embryonic stem cells directly from adult cells. In fact, the new method may actually prove superior to embryo-destructive alternatives. This is the biggest stem cell advance since James Thomson became the first scientist to isolate embryonic stem cells, less than a decade ago [in 1998].

It is a new study by Thomson himself that has caused the present stir, but this time Thomson is not alone. Accounts of independent research by two separate teams of scientists were published [in 2007]—one in the journal *Cell* and one in the journal *Science*—documenting the production of pluripotent

Ryan T. Anderson, "The End of the Stem-Cell Wars," November 27, 2007. FrontPage Magazine.com. Copyright © 2007 FrontPageMagazine.com. Reproduced by permission.

human stem cells without using embryos or eggs or cloning or any morally questionable method at all.

The new technique is so promising that Ian Wilmut announced that he would no longer seek to clone humans. Wilmut, you may remember, is the scientist who cloned Dolly the sheep [in 1996]. He recently sought and received a license from the British government to attempt to clone human embryos for research purposes. Now, citing the new technique, he has abandoned his plans.

Background of the Debate

It was only in 1998 that Thomson succeeded in isolating human embryonic stem cells. Though other types of human stem cells were known at the time (some were even in clinical trials), embryonic stem cells were thought to be the holy grail because they were believed to be more flexible. They were "pluripotent"—capable, in theory, of developing into any type of body tissue—whereas so-called adult stem cells were thought to be useful for forming a narrower range of tissue types. The problem with producing embryonic stem cells was that human embryos—nascent human beings—had to be destroyed in the process.

Even now, nine years later [in 2007], embryonic stem cells are thought by many scientists to have greater potential than other types. This reputation persists even though adult stem cells are already used in therapies to treat several diseases and are being tested in hundreds of clinical trials, while not a single embryonic stem cell therapy exists, even in trials.

Embryo destruction . . . has become not only unnecessary but also less efficient than the alternatives.

As anyone familiar with reparative medicine knows, immune rejection is one of the tallest hurdles to clear. The promise of cloning was that therapies could be produced using hu-

man embryos cloned directly from the patient—thus resulting in a genetic match. Cloning, it was said, would also provide an unlimited supply of human embryos. But many people thought human cloning with the sole intention to kill crossed an ethical line. In addition, human cloning would require an enormous number of human eggs—which could be obtained only by subjecting donors to painful and potentially danger-ous hormonal-stimulation procedures. The fear was that likely "donors" would be poor women undergoing a distasteful pro-cedure solely for the fee.

On August 9, 2001, President [George W.] Bush waded into this morass. He issued an executive order that opened human embryonic stem cell research to federal funding for the first time ever. The order also restricted that funding, however, to research using existing embryonic stem cell lines: No more embryos would be created and destroyed for taxpayer-funded research. (Contrary to popular belief, Bush's order did not *ban* anything.) Opposition was fierce, but Bush stood firm.

Search for Alternatives

Amid this controversy, a number of scientists discussed pos-sible alternative sources of embryonic stem cells. William Hurlbut, a professor at Stanford and a member of the President's Council on Bioethics, proposed Altered Nuclear Transfer, a process that produced nonembryonic tumor-like entities that could then be harvested for the equivalent of em-bryonic stem cells. Some ethicists weren't fully sold, fearing that the tumor-like entities might be deformed embryos. Hurlbut's proposal was then modified, using oocyte cytoplasm to directly reprogram a cell's nucleus to make it pluripotent. Still, some critics were unconvinced. Finally, using mice, a Japanese scientist, Shinya Yamanaka, showed that he could create embryonic stem cells directly from adult cells, and within less than a year his study was replicated and signifi-

cantly expanded by two separate research groups. Yamanaka went to work to make it happen with human cells.

But outside the scientific community, conventional wisdom held that these alternative sources, while interesting, were being proposed only to provide Bush with political cover during the waning years of his presidency. As soon as a new president was inaugurated, federal funds would flow into human cloning and embryo-destructive research. Or so the story went.

That expectation has now been shattered. Whether or not the next president shares Bush's pro-life convictions, it is highly unlikely that taxpayer funds will go to support embryo destruction, which has become not only unnecessary but also less efficient than the alternatives. That's the story coming out of *Cell* and *Science*.

In *Cell*, Yamanaka announces that the pluripotent stem cell-producing technique he used on mouse cells works with human cells. The resulting cells—called induced pluripotent stem cells, or iPS cells—are functionally identical to human embryonic stem cells: They possess all of the same properties. The difference is simply in the method of their production.

This new production technique is possible because the difference between a stem cell and an adult cell is not a matter of genetics but of epigenetics: which genes are expressed, how, and to what degree. Different cells have the same genes, expressed differently. So scientists had been searching for a way to remodel the gene expression of adult cells to transform them into stem cells. Yamanaka's team discovered a collection of four genes—Oct3/4, Sox2, Klf4, and c-Myc—that does precisely this. When introduced into adult cells, these genes directly reprogram the cell to a pluripotent state.

A Real Breakthrough

I asked Maureen Condic, professor of neurobiology and anatomy at the University of Utah School of Medicine, about

these cells. "Direct reprogramming of adult cells to pluripotent stem cells is one of the most significant scientific findings of the last quarter century," she said. "This approach holds tremendous promise for advancing our scientific understanding of stem cells and for advancing the study of regenerative medicine. However, there are concerns regarding the safety of iPS cells for human therapies, due to the use of viral vectors that integrate into the cell's DNA, potentially causing dangerous mutations, and to the use of c-Myc, a gene that is associated with some forms of human cancer."

Yamanaka himself notes these pitfalls, but indicates that they should be surmountable: His technique works even when you take c-Myc out of the mix and use only the other three genes (though it achieves its results at a less efficient rate). Moreover, Yamanaka notes that integration of the virus into the DNA will not reduce the usefulness of induced pluripotent stem cells for study of human diseases in the laboratory, and that other nonviral means of introducing the reprogramming factors into cells are likely to be sufficient to generate iPS cells.

The new technique produces patient-specific stem cells with all the benefits of stem cells from embryos, but without the production and destruction of human embryos.

The Thomson approach described in *Science* avoided some of these drawbacks by using no c-Myc and optimizing the safety of the induced pluripotent stem cells from the start. His team used a different group of genes—Oct4, Sox2, Nanog, and Lin28—to achieve the same end: direct reprogramming of adult human cells to the pluripotent state. Thomson's technique is also noteworthy because it uses a lentivirus to introduce the gene group, which is the safest of retroviral integration methods. Work still needs to be done to ensure that viral

vectors do not introduce dangerous mutations, but the scientists I spoke with thought this would be achievable with minimal delay.

What does all of this mean? James Thomson explains it best in his *Science* paper:

> The human iPS cells described here meet the defining criteria we originally proposed for human embryonic stem cells, with the significant exception that the iPS cells are not derived from embryos. Similar to human embryonic stem cells, human iPS cells should prove useful for studying the development and function of human tissues, for discovering and testing new drugs, and for transplantation medicine. For transplantation therapies based on these cells, with the exception of autoimmune diseases, patient-specific iPS cell lines should largely eliminate the concern of immune rejection.

In short: The new technique produces patient-specific stem cells with all the benefits of stem cells from embryos, but without the production and destruction of human embryos or the use of human eggs.

Because induced pluripotent stem cells, created from a patient's own body, are a perfect genetic match, they should prove especially useful for both the study of diseases and the development of treatments. Thomson notes, "For drug development, human iPS cells should make it easier to generate panels of cell lines that more closely reflect the genetic diversity of a population, and should make it possible to generate cell lines from individuals predisposed to specific diseases."

Wilmut, of Dolly the sheep fame, agrees. Comparing his cloning methods with Yamanaka's, he said, "The work which was described from Japan of using a technique to change cells from a patient directly into stem cells without making an embryo has got so much more potential."

Challenges Ahead

Nonetheless, there are serious challenges to overcome before pluripotent stem cells—whatever their source—will be ready for clinical therapies. All pluripotent stem cells carry a risk of tumor formation. And no one has yet figured out how to convert these stem cells into transplantable cells usable for therapies. Markus Grompe, professor in the department of molecular and medical genetics at the Oregon Health and Science University, director of the Oregon Stem Cell Center, and a board member of the International Society for Stem Cell Research, told me that "the therapeutic potential of all human pluripotent stem cells, including those generated by direct reprogramming, remains uncertain. No immediate cures should be expected from human pluripotent stem cell–based therapy, either embryo-derived or iPS. First, the tumor risk of such cells must be harnessed, and second, the efficient conversion to transplantable cells must be mastered."

But scientists are hopeful that these hurdles will be overcome. Grompe points out that stem cells have important uses beyond therapy, and for these uses, too,

> iPS cells are clearly superior to embryo-derived stem cells. They can be used to study how human organs and tissues form. And the insights gained are likely to lead to the development of new drugs and strategies to benefit human health. Direct reprogramming techniques make it possible to generate pluripotent cells from specific individuals with particular diseases. For example, it will be possible to make pluripotent stem cells from children with Fanconi's anemia, a devastating genetic disease, and study the effects of candidate drugs on the formation of human blood. Another example, favored by Ian Wilmut, is motor neuron disease (Lou Gehrig's disease). Here it will be of interest to examine the formation of nerves and motor neurons from patients with the actual disease, in an attempt to discover ways to help the cells sur-

vive and function better. These kinds of experiments are now immediately possible and will likely be the first application of iPS cells.

Thus, iPS cells may very well help us discover therapies for some of the most daunting genetic diseases. And they should be able to do so at last without controversy.

Ethical Concerns Allayed

The ethicists I spoke with had only praise for the new developments. While some Catholic moral theologians had previously worried that reprogramming methods "mimicked conception" and might produce disabled embryos, the new technique should alleviate all fears. Concerns that scientists might "go too far back" and reprogram a cell to a totipotent stage—making an actual embryo, not a stem cell—are quickly settled once one understands the science. To be an embryo requires not only a particular nuclear state, but also certain organizational factors that the oocyte cytoplasm provides. But no egg or cytoplasm is used in this method. Furthermore, two of the genes used for reprogramming—Nanog and Sox2—are never found in embryos, only in stem cells. Their expression in reprogramming precludes totipotency.

When I asked Father Thomas Berg, the executive director of the Westchester Institute for Ethics and the Human Person, about this concern, he replied, "From a Catholic perspective, reprogramming clears the bar in terms of reasonable concern for human dignity in biotech research: Never at any point in the process of reprogramming is there ever a danger of involving—even accidentally we might say—techniques that could bring about a human embryo, as would happen in cloning. The science of pluripotent stem cell research can move forward toward therapies and cures in a manner that is free of any ethical concerns."

What about all of those antiscience religious fanatics who used to scold about "playing God"? They don't exist. They're a

media-conjured fantasy. Of all the many people I have talked with about stem cells, none has ever expressed any antiscience or antimedicine inclinations.

Scientists [now have] a better method of producing embryonic stem cells while retaining our nation's commitment to the equal and inherent dignity of all human beings.

Princeton's legal philosopher Robert P. George, who also serves on the President's Council on Bioethics, told me, "From the beginning we have been arguing that we must do everything we can to advance the cause of stem cell science but without sacrificing our respect for nascent human life and the principle of the inherent and equal dignity of each and every member of the human family. This latest news just goes to show that it really is possible."

It also is illustrative of the politics of science. Had a President [Al] Gore or a President [John] Kerry allowed the science to go forward without regard for moral principle, it would have set a terrible precedent. A Gore or Kerry presidency would have bestowed federal blessing and taxpayer funds on laboratory work predicated on the assumption that embryonic human beings can be treated as spare parts and that cloning to kill is acceptable.

Vindication for Pro-Lifers

But because President Bush stood his ground, we have avoided that moral catastrophe. Had Bush lost either election, or had he caved to pressure from those who slandered him as "antiscience," it is very possible that the new method of stem cell production—the new gold standard, in all likelihood—would never have been found. Most likely, science and the public would have accommodated themselves to the mass production and mass killing of human embryos.

Indeed, it is not Bush alone, but the entire pro-life movement, that has been vindicated. For the petition-signers and the direct-mail organizers, the philosophers and the scientists who have defended the sanctity of human life, the *Cell* and *Science* stories come as a reward. When I spoke with Robert George, he praised Leon Kass, the former chairman of the President's Council, together with William Hurlbut, as the driving intellectual force against embryo-killing and in favor of finding alternative methods of obtaining pluripotent stem cells. "All along," George reports, "it was Dr. Kass who said that reprogramming methods would, if pursued vigorously, enable us to realize the full benefits of stem cell science while respecting human dignity."

George downplays his own role in shaping the president's thinking. After Congress passed a bill funding embryo-destructive stem cell research, Bush sought counsel. His approval ratings were in the cellar, and the general public largely supported the bill. Shortly before announcing his response to the legislation, the president invited George and Grompe to the Oval Office to discuss it with him. George presented the scientific and philosophical case for respecting the human embryo, while Grompe assured the president that alternatives such as reprogramming, if given time, would win the day. The president agreed and announced his veto. He was right.

And Congress was wrong. Considering the realities of Washington, it is no surprise that the pro–embryo-destruction forces in the House of Representatives actually teamed up to defeat a bill that would have funded research on reprogramming, which they dismissed as a distraction. President Bush then issued another executive order, this one instructing the National Institutes of Health [NIH] to promote reprogramming research. As it turns out, the breakthrough Thomson study was partially funded by NIH.

Stem cell research wasn't a prime issue during the 2000 campaign. Politically, the controversy wasn't yet ripe, though it

became so just months into Bush's first term. Similarly, now, we don't know what the next biotech breakthrough will be. Whatever it is, we can be certain that some people will demand we pursue it. Having political leaders of principle who insist on ethical standards in scientific research, then, is always of the utmost importance.

At present, people on all sides of the old stem cell debate should be able to celebrate. The recent news gives scientists a better method of producing embryonic stem cells while retaining our nation's commitment to the equal and inherent dignity of all human beings. Richard Doerflinger of the U.S. Conference of Catholic Bishops pointed out the happy irony: "The scientist who gave us human embryonic stem cell research has helped find the way to go beyond embryo-destructive research, and in response to these new findings, the scientist who gave us cloning tells us that the cloning agenda is on the way to being obsolete."

Despite Advances Embryonic, Not Adult, Stem Cells Are More Valuable

Jonathan D. Moreno and Sam Berger

Jonathan D. Moreno is a professor at the University of Pennsylvania and director of the Center for Biomedical Ethics at the University of Virginia. He is also a senior fellow at the Center for American Progress and director of the Progressive Bioethics Initiative. Sam Berger is a researcher at the Center for American Progress.

Despite recent scientific advancements, the limitations on embryonic stem cell research should be lifted. Amniotic stem cells are very promising, but they do not replace embryonic stem cells. Congress should pass the Stem Cell Research Enhancement Act to ensure that embryonic stem cell research moves forward unobstructed by political concerns.

Since President [George W.] Bush's veto of the Stem Cell Research Enhancement Act [in 2006], scientists have made great research strides in the field. But as much as stem cell research has advanced scientifically, politically, things have stayed the same.

Federally funded stem cell researchers are still limited to only 21 older and potentially less useful stem cell lines, while scientists in other countries have access to a newer and larger

variety. Recent scientific advances, including deriving stem cells from eggs and amniotic fluid, show the promise of the research. But they cannot serve as replacements for robust support for embryonic stem cell research.

Comprehensive Support

Stem cell research should not be pursued in bits and pieces; comprehensive support is necessary to truly advance the science. Congress will be bringing the Stem Cell Research Enhancement Act back up for a vote [in 2007], in the hopes of giving scientists access to the best tools we have in the race for life-saving cures.

Politicians tend to characterize the stem cell debate as embryonic versus adult stem cells, but the scientific reality is far different. Scientists do not think of research using embryonic and adult stem cells as separate enterprises, but rather as different tools in regenerative medicine—the use of cells from a variety of sources to cure diseases, learn more about human development, and more effectively develop drugs.

Researchers understand that different types of cells will prove useful for different purposes. Certain diseases or injuries may require treatment with adult or [umbilical] cord blood stem cells, while others will respond better to treatments with embryonic stem cells. Most importantly, research on one type of stem cell helps scientists working with *all* types of cells; as adult stem cell researcher Dr. David Scadden commented, "adult stem cell therapies will be bettered by the study of embryonic stem cells." Conversely, hindering any type of stem cell research will slow research in other areas as well.

The recent announcement by scientists that they have discovered stem cells in amniotic fluid is very promising news. These new stem cells can be safely obtained through either amniocentesis or from the placenta, grow at a fast rate, become many of the cells in the human body, and provide a genetic match for the newborn child, thus reducing the chance of tissue rejection.

Embryonic Stem Cells Still Valuable

Yet, as the scientists who conducted the research made clear, they will not replace embryonic stem cells. There are still questions regarding how many different types of cells these new stem cells can become; stem cell scientist Dr. Robert Lanza commented that, "the [new stem cells] can clearly generate a broad range of important cell types, but they may not do as many tricks as embryonic stem cells." Unlike embryonic stem cells, which can become any type of cell in the human body, the amniotic-fluid cells appear to be multipotent; they can become many types, but not all.

Amniotic-fluid stem cells will also not be as helpful for answering questions about early human development, which scientists consider to be one of the most important potentials of embryonic stem cell research. And it will take years for scientists to reproduce these new stem cells and determine how to use them clinically.

In short, embryonic stem cells are still the most medically promising type of stem cells.

Meanwhile, scientists also recently announced that they had derived stem cells through parthenogenesis, which coaxes an unfertilized egg into developing as if it were fertilized. The cells derived from this process appear to have similar characteristics to embryonic stem cells, but unfortunately suffer from several drawbacks. Such cells have two sets of genes from the egg, instead of one set from the egg and one set from the sperm. This altered set of genes could lead to poor cell growth, abnormal cell development or cancer, and increases the risk of duplicate mutant genes that could cause additional problems. Also, parthenogenesis could only be used to develop stem cells that are genetic matches for women, and attempts to develop stem cells from sperm have proven more difficult.

83

Scientists will need additional time and resources to determine how to efficiently isolate and manipulate new types of stem cells, but they continue to make tremendous advances in the use of embryonic stem cells *now*. Researchers have used embryonic stem cells in laboratory animals to treat paralysis, slow vision loss, and reverse some of the symptoms of Parkinson's disease. They have used human embryonic stem cells to create cardiovascular precursor cells that could lead to treatments for heart diseases, T-cells that could lead to a cure for AIDS, and insulin-secreting cells that could lead to a cure for diabetes. And there is a ready supply of 400,000 excess embryos stored in fertility clinics around the country.

In short, embryonic stem cells are still the most medically promising type of stem cells because of their ability to differentiate into any cell in the human body. Recent advances in embryonic stem cell research coupled with the discovery of new sources of stem cells only underscore the potential of this life-saving research.

The American people have also demonstrated tremendous support for this science—56 percent want Congress to pass the Stem Cell Research Enhancement Act, and during the 2006 midterm election supporters of embryonic stem cell research won 62 percent of their races against opponents of the research. Congress already passed this legislation once with broad bipartisan support, only to see President Bush veto it. With all the scientific advances since then, one might expect to see this legislation advance as well.

Embryonic Stem Cells Should Not Be Used for Cloning

Wendy Wright

Wendy Wright is a contributing writer for Concerned Women for America, the nation's largest public policy women's organization, bringing Biblical principles into all levels of public policy.

Advocates for cloning believe the technique will push medicine toward curing diseases. What most advocates fail to mention are the abnormalities and other physical defects that go along with both therapeutic and reproductive cloning. Along with the physical affects, cloning defies human dignity by disregarding an individual's rights, identity, and uniqueness. Reproductive cloning has already been condemned by the United Nations and should be banned altogether.

Cloning: Medical Miracle or Human Hubris?

Should human beings be cloned? With a Brave New World advancing quickly upon us, each new announcement of cloned animals, chimeras and human embryos finds scientists, ethicists, politicians and citizens trying to answer the ultimate question: whether what *can* be done, *should* be done.

The majority of Americans, and people around the world, are repulsed at the idea of creating identical replicas of human beings. Proponents of cloning, however, are working to change this.

Wendy Wright, "Cloning: Medical Miracle or Human Hubris?" Concerned Women for America, June 17, 2003. www.cwfa.org. Reproduced with permission.

Tapping into the natural compassion for victims of disease and handicaps, the bio-tech industry is presenting cloning as a potential avenue to healing. The industry has divided the debate over cloning into two realms: reproductive and therapeutic.

No disease or disability in humans has yet been cured through the use of embryonic stem cells.

What is Cloning?

Cloning is the creation of a being that is genetically identical to its "parent." The common method, used with Dolly the sheep, is to extract the nucleus from an egg, inject a cell containing DNA from the donor, and then give the egg a shock of electricity to stimulate cell division.

In "reproductive cloning," the new life is implanted in a surrogate mother and allowed to grow and be born. "Therapeutic cloning" uses the same method, but rather than implanting the clone and allowing it to be born, researchers use the embryo as raw material for experiments or to scavenge for parts, such as skin, muscle, nerve or brain cells. A "therapeutic clone" is no different from a "reproductive clone"—only the researchers' intent on what to do with the clone changes.

The goal of therapeutic cloning is to obtain embryonic stem cells that, in theory, may develop into any kind of cell or body tissue. Scientists hope to use the stem cells to treat diseases. Since the embryo's tissue would be genetically identical to the donor, it could conceivably avoid the problem of tissue rejection. However, in animals, it often takes 100 or more eggs to get one viable clone.[1] (After receiving hormone injections for days for in vitro fertilization, women will typically produce 10 to 15 eggs.[2]) Further, the success of these treatments is speculative. No disease or disability in humans has yet been cured through the use of embryonic stem cells.

The High Failure Rate of Cloning

Advanced Cell Technology, a Massachusetts bio-tech firm, claims it created one human embryo that grew into six cells before dying. Embryonic stem cells are not present at this early stage. Most of the eggs in the research died without dividing once. Despite the headlines that a human clone had been created, objective researchers noted there was more hype than substance behind the announcement, perhaps to gain attention and funding for the bio-tech firm.[3]

Regardless, Dr. Tanja Dominko, an Advanced Cell Technology researcher, said her work on cloning monkey embryos (before she joined ACT) resulted in gross abnormalities in most embryos, which died within five days—too early for stem cells to appear.[4] Though they look healthy, Dr. Dominko said, a high percentage of cloned monkey embryos are really a "gallery of horrors" within.[5]

Most efforts fail, even in species that have at one time or another been cloned. Researchers who have occasional success cloning one species, like cows, are finding failure with others, like dogs. Cloning success is the exception, not the rule.[6]

Dr. Wilmut, the British scientist who successfully cloned Dolly the sheep, said, in general, just 1 to 4 percent of efforts *in a species where cloning has worked* result in the birth of a live animal. That, he said, indicates that cloning appears to create serious abnormalities in almost all embryos.[7]

Severe problems, including defects in the heart, lungs and other organs, are suffered by half of all clones of large mammals, like sheep and cows. Most die before they are born. Others that survive die suddenly and mysteriously weeks or months after birth.[8]

Reproductive Cloning Defies Human Dignity

While reproductive cloning of humans is nearly universally condemned, rogue scientists and their benefactors continue to

attempt it. Rep. Dave Weldon's (R-Florida) "Human Cloning Prohibition Act of 2001" (H.R. 2505) would ban all human cloning, while permitting the replication of DNA, cells or tissues (but not embryos) for experimental or therapeutic purposes. It passed in the House of Representatives, but Majority Leader Tom Daschle (D-South Dakota) continues to delay a vote in the Senate.

The United Nations condemned reproductive cloning in 1997 when it unanimously adopted the Universal Declaration on the Human Genome and Human Rights. This states, "Practices which are contrary to human dignity, such as reproductive cloning of human beings, shall not be permitted." In 2000, the United Kingdom passed a ban on reproductive cloning, but allowed for therapeutic cloning.

This revulsion for the cloning of humans is a natural response to the utter disregard for human dignity. Cloning inherently treats people as "replacements" or "extras." This defies the uniqueness of each individual, using technology to manipulate and control human beings. It would create a class of humans deprived of a clear identity, parents and family.

Therapeutic cloning, or creating clones to harvest their cells, was also roundly condemned until scientists and their fundraisers promoted the idea that the end (helping patients) justifies the means (creating humans to use for experiments or parts).

Scientists who claim to be helping grieving family or friends by resurrecting a loved one through cloning are committing fraud. Experiments to create cloned humans carry unimagined, horrific physical risks to the clone and to the woman who carries it. Most animal embryo clones are horribly deformed and die. The few that live long enough to be implanted in an animal's uterus die soon afterward. The anomalies that have survived to birth are prone to genetic de-

fects. A cloned lamb born soon after Dolly displayed such severe respiratory problems that within a few weeks she was euthanized. An autopsy revealed that her lungs had not developed properly.[9]

Cloned cows, sheep, goats, and mice often have over-sized internal organs, limbs, and overall body, and the newborns are sickly. The large fetuses cause a risk to the mother during delivery. The dismal results of animal cloning have convinced many scientists that it is unthinkable to clone a human.[10]

Beyond the physical problems, the cloned human has no defined rights. Who is the parent—the donor or the scientist? Who is responsible when things go wrong? Could a cloned human be killed if he or she were found to be defective or unwanted? Would a clone be treated differently than humans with two biological parents? When would a clone have legal or human rights? What if a living or deceased person is cloned without his or her knowledge or consent?

It is wrong to treat a human as something that can be replaced, and it is wrong to treat another human as a mere substitute.

Genetic Defects

Therapeutic cloning, or creating clones to harvest their cells, was also roundly condemned until scientists and their fundraisers promoted the idea that the end (helping patients) justifies the means (creating humans to use for experiments or parts).

However, cloned (or even adult) stem cells would not be useful unless the genetic defects were corrected before they were injected back into a patient. "It's one thing to re-create a pancreas, but if you have to regenerate from diseased tissue, the gene is still defective," says Inder M. Verma of the Salk Institute for Biological Studies in San Diego, California. "You have to correct the defect; otherwise cloning will get you what you started out with."[11]

There is Hope for Patients

Since the excuse for allowing scientists to pursue therapeutic cloning is to obtain valuable stem cells, if there are other—or better—sources for stem cells, then the dangers and indignities of cloning cannot be justified. And, there are much better sources.

Stem cells from adults and umbilical cord blood are already being used to treat numerous kinds of cancer and diseases, to regenerate muscle tissue, and to form cartilage and bone tissue. Adult stem cells bypass the problem of donor rejection, as the patient is the donor, and are a quicker source for stem cells than the laborious, unnecessary step of creating an embryo. There is no need to go through the immoral and dangerous process of cloning when stem cells can be safely obtained directly from the patient.

Additionally, a "miracle" stem cell has been discovered. Mesenchymal stem cells, or MSCs, are found in adult bone marrow. Embryonic stem cells cannot be directed to become the kind of cell desired and, more ominously, can grow into tumors. However, when MSCs are injected, they only seem to go to the patient's damaged areas, turning into appropriately needed muscle, blood vessels, cartilage, bone and other tissue. They do not carry markers that lead to rejection. The cells are so safe they can be transplanted between different species. A single bone-marrow donation could treat 10,000 people or more.[12]

Many diseases and disabilities are the result of cells dying. Donated stem cells can replace the damaged ones. Another source for cell regeneration are drugs that stimulate the brain and other organs to grow new cells and repair themselves. Drugs do not present the problem of rejection by a patient's immune system, and they do not require invasive surgery. Epogen, a drug produced by Amgen, fights anemia by using a human protein to stimulate the body to produce red blood

cells. Another protein developed by Curis Inc. stimulates bone growth, which can treat fractures that do not heal.[13]

Why a Ban on Reproductive Cloning Won't Work

Sen. Tom Daschle (D-South Dakota) and other politicians say they support a ban on reproductive cloning, but not a ban on therapeutic. Both the United Nations' resolution and England's ban allow for therapeutic cloning. But can a partial ban work?

The only way to uphold such a ban would be to forcefully abort a woman carrying a human clone. Barring that, how would politicians deal with a clone who escapes detection and is born? Since the clone had no right to be born, would this new person have any legal or human rights, or even be recognized as a human being?

Those working on the front lines recognize that the demarcation between reproductive and therapeutic cloning is easy to cross. Advanced Cell Technology's president Michael West, while arguing for therapeutic cloning, has written that reproductive cloning is "unwarranted at this time" and should be restricted—that is, "until the safety and ethical issues surrounding it are resolved."[14]

Severino Antinori, a scientist who claims he will create a cloned human being soon, stated that reproductive cloning is therapeutic cloning. He argues that infertility is a disease, and the cure, or therapy, is cloning.[15]

Cloning is High-Tech Slavery

Cloning causes people to view human beings as commodities, something to be mass-produced. Cloning supporters attempt to imitate God, but their intentions are warped from His because they desire to produce beings that are distinctly *not* unique. If clones were distinct, individual, one-of-a-kind— traits of all humans, including identical twins—the goal of

cloning supporters would be thwarted. Noble excuses cannot disguise the reprehensible mindset that views human beings as replaceable.

Slavery treats a class of people as sub-human. Depraved philosophies like that of the Nazi experimenters view people only in the context of how their body parts can be exploited. Cloning is the modern-day version of history's corrupt endeavors. The act of cloning views human life as something to be manipulated, used, and disposed of. It endangers the life and health of the offspring, most of which will die in the process, while the few survivors will have deformities and suffer indignities. If we allow technology and rogue scientists to determine the worth, relationships and use of people, civilization as we know it will suffer.

End Notes

1. Gina Kolata, "A Thick Line Between Theory and Therapy, as Shown With Mice," *The New York Times*, December 18, 2001, D3.

2. Andrew Pollack, "Use of Cloning to Tailor Treatment Has Big Hurdles, Including Cost," *The New York Times*, December 18, 2001, D2.

3. Michael Lemonick, "Just Cloning Around," *Time* magazine, December 2, 2001.

4. Gina Kolata, "In Cloning, Failure Far Exceeds Success," *The New York Times*, December 11, 2001.

5. Sylvia Pagan Westphal, "Cloned Monkey Embryos Are a 'Gallery of Horrors,'" *New Scientist*, December 12, 2001.

6. Op. cit.

7. Ibid.

8. Rick Weiss, "Clone Defects Point to Need for 2 Genetic Parents," *Washington Post*, May 10, 1999, A1.

9. John Travis, "Dolly Was Lucky: Scientists warn that cloning is too dangerous for people," *Science News* Vol. 160, October 20, 2001, 250.

10. Ibid.

11. Carol Ezzell, "Stem Cell Showstopper?" *Scientific American*, November 15, 2001.

12. "Stem Cell Transplant Boost," *BBC News*, December 12, 2001.

13. Andrew Pollack, "Drugs to Spur New Cells, and Without the Politics," *The New York Times*, December 13, 2001.

14. Denise Gellene and Elizabeth Mehren, "Human-Cloning Research Firm Received Federal Aid," *Los Angeles Times*, November 29, 2001.

15. Author's notes, National Academy of Sciences panel, Washington, D.C., August 2001.

The Embryo Glut Has Unexpected Consequences in the Stem Cell Debate

Liza Mundy

Liza Mundy is a staff writer for the Washington Post.

There is an excess of embryos because of the growing popularity of in vitro fertilization treatments. This excess of embryos—more than four hundred thousand, according to one estimate—has forced many people to reevaluate their own opinions on life and death and reproductive freedom.

Janis Elspas is a mother of four. Unlike most parents, she had three of her children simultaneously. The nine-year-old triplets were born in 1997 after Elspas underwent a series of in vitro fertilization [IVF] treatments for infertility. Her oldest child, 10, is the happy result of a prior IVF treatment round. Elspas worked hard to get her children, and is grateful to have them. But four, thanks very much, are plenty. The problem is that Elspas also has 14 embryos left over from the treatment that produced her 10-year-old. The embryos are stored in liquid nitrogen at a California frozen storage facility—she is not entirely sure where—while Elspas and her husband ponder what to do with them.

Give them away to another couple, to gestate and bear? Her own children's full biological siblings—raised in a differ-

ent family? Donate them to scientific research? Let them . . . finally . . . lapse? It is, she and her husband find, an intractable problem, one for which there is no satisfactory answer. So what they have done—thus far—is nothing. Nothing, that is, but agonize.

"I don't have the heart to thaw them," says Elspas, who works as media relations director for a multi-birth networking group called the Triplet Connection. "But then again, I don't have the will to do something with them."

This embryo glut is forcing many people to reconsider whatever they thought they thought about issues such as life and death and choice and reproductive freedom.

A Glut of Embryos

Elspas is by no means alone, either in having frozen human embryos she and her husband must eventually figure out what to do with, or in the moral paralysis she feels, surveying the landscape of available choices. In fact, she is part of an explosively growing group. In 2002, the Society for Assisted Reproductive Technology—the research arm for U.S. fertility doctors—decided to find out how many unused embryos had accumulated in the nation's 430 fertility clinics. The Rand consulting group, hired to do a head count, concluded that 400,000 frozen embryos existed—a staggering number, twice as large as previous estimates. Given that hundreds of thousands of IVF treatment rounds have since been performed, it seems fair to estimate that by now the number of embryos in limbo in the United States alone is closer to half a million.

This embryo glut is forcing many people to reconsider whatever they thought they thought about issues such as life and death and choice and reproductive freedom. It's a dilemma that has been quietly building: The first American IVF baby was born in 1981, less than a decade after *Roe v. Wade*

[overturning laws that restricted abortion] was decided. Thanks in part to *Roe*, fertility medicine in this country developed in an atmosphere of considerable reproductive freedom (read: very little government oversight), meaning, among other things, that responsibility for embryo disposition rests squarely with patients. The number of IVF rounds, or "cycles," has grown to the point that in 2003 about 123,000 cycles were performed, to help some of the estimated 1 in 7 American couples who have difficulty conceiving naturally. Early on, it proved relatively easy to freeze a lab-created human embryo— which unlike, say, hamburger meat, can be frozen, and thawed, and refrozen, and thawed, and then used. (To be precise, the technical term is "pre-embryo," or "conceptus"; a fertilized egg is not considered an embryo until about two weeks of development, and IVF embryos are frozen well before this point.) Over time—as fertility drugs have gotten more powerful and lab procedures more efficient—it has become possible to coax more and more embryos into being during the average cycle. Moreover, as doctors transfer fewer embryos back into patients, in an effort to reduce multiple births, more of the embryos made are subsequently frozen.

And so, far from going away, the accumulation of human embryos is likely to grow, and grow, and grow. And in growing, the embryo overstock is likely to change—or at least complicate—the way we collectively think about human life at its earliest stages, and morally what is the right thing to do with it. At some point, embryos may alter or even explode the reproductive landscape: It is IVF embryos, after all, that are at the center of the nation's stem cell debate, which itself has prompted a new national conversation about life and reproductive liberty, creating new alliances as well as schisms. In 2001, as one of his first major domestic policy decisions, [President] George W. Bush banned federal funding for labs developing new stem cell lines using leftover IVF embryos; then in May 2005, the U.S. House of Representatives passed a

bill approving funding for stem cell research using these same embryos, setting the stage for an eventual conservative show-down. In the course of this debate, embryos have emerged as another tool for truly hardline conservatives looking for new ways to beat back abortion rights. Like "fetal rights" laws that seemingly protect unborn children from acts of homicide, "embryo rights" are being waved about as a weapon in the assault on abortion rights, as anti-abortion lawmakers talk about seizing control over frozen embryo stores; limiting the creation of new embryos; or both.

A new demographic is wrestling with questions initially posed by contraception and abortion.

The Disposition Decision

But the impact of the embryo is also taking place on a more subtle and personal level. The glut's very existence illuminates how the newest reproductive technologies are complicating questions about life; issues that many people thought they had resolved are being revived and reconsidered, in a different emotional context. As with ultrasound technology—which permits parents to visualize a fetus in utero—IVF allows many patients to form an emotional attachment to a form of human life that is very early, it's true, but still life, and still human. People bond with photos of three-day-old, eight-cell embryos. They ardently wish for them to grow into children. The experience can be transforming: "I was like, 'I created these things, I feel a sense of responsibility for them,'" is how one IVF patient put it. Describing herself as staunchly pro-choice, this patient found that she could not rest until she located a person—actually, two people—willing to bring her excess embryos to term. The presence of embryos for whom (for which?) they feel a certain undefined moral responsibility presents tens of thousands of Americans with a dilemma for which nothing—nothing—has prepared them.

A new demographic is wrestling with questions initially posed by contraception and abortion. A world away from the exigencies, mitigating circumstances, and carefully honed ideologies that have grown up in and around U.S. abortion clinics, it is people like Janis Elspas who are being called upon to think, hard, about when life begins, and when it is—or is not—right to terminate it. They are in this position, ironically enough, not because they don't want a family, but precisely because they do. Among the nation's growing ranks of IVF patients, deciding the fate of frozen embryos is known as the "disposition decision," and it is one of the hardest decisions patients face, so unexpectedly problematic that many decide, in the end, to punt, a choice that is only going to make the glut bigger, the moral problem more looming and unresolved.

Organizations to Contact

American Enterprise Institute (AEI)
1150 Seventeenth St. NW, Washington, DC   20036
(202) 862-5800 • fax: (202) 862-7177
Web site: www.aei.org

Founded in 1943, the American Enterprise Institute for Public Policy Research is a conservative think tank that provides research and commentary on issues of government, politics, economics, and social welfare. AEI sponsors research on these topics as well as conferences, seminars, and symposia on issues of national importance. AEI publishes books, monographs, periodicals, a monthly newsletter, and the *American*, a bimonthly magazine covering current political events and controversies. AEI scholars have published a number of articles and editorials exploring the debate over embryonic stem cell research. The AEI Web site features a number of speeches as well as government testimony by AEI scholars regarding key issues of the day, including the ethics of federally funded embryonic stem cell research.

Americans for Cures Foundation
550 S. California Ave., Suite 330, Palo Alto, CA   94306
(650) 812-9303 • fax: (650) 833-0105
e-mail: inform@americansforcures.org
Web site: www.americansforcures.org

Americans for Cures is a nonpartisan, pro–stem cell research advocacy group that distributes factual information about stem cell research, addresses inaccurate and politically motivated attacks, supports like-minded groups and scientists, and encourages decision makers to fund research. The foundation also supports legislative action to advance and protect stem cell research and hosts community forums to explain the benefits of research and disseminate scientific facts to concerned

citizens. For scientists, the group hosts seminars, symposia, and conferences to provide a forum for stem cell experts to exchange ideas and information on the latest research and scientific progress. Its Web site provides a plethora of facts about stem cell research and information about the latest breakthroughs in the field.

Center for American Progress (CAP)
1333 H St. NW, 10th Floor, Washington, DC   20005
(202) 682-1611 • fax: (202) 682-1867
e-mail: progress@americanprogress.org
Web site: www.americanprogress.org

Established in 2003, the Center for American Progress is a progressive think tank that puts forth policy ideas on a wide range of political and social issues. CAP focuses on four main areas: delivering universal health care, creating economic opportunities for all, supporting the development of alternative fuels, and restoring America's leadership abroad. The center sponsors panels, symposia, and conferences to advocate for progressive policies on domestic and national security issues. One of the center's primary goals on the domestic front has been lifting the Bush administration ban on federal funding for embryonic stem cell research. In recent papers such as "New Possibilities for Stem Cell Research" and "Disposition of Frozen Embryos," experts report on the latest breakthroughs on stem cell research and ponder the ethical and moral questions surrounding embryonic stem cell research.

Coalition for the Advancement of Medical Research (CAMR)
2021 K St. NW, Suite 305, Washington, DC   20006
(202) 725-0339
e-mail: camresearch@yahoo.com
Web site: www.camradvocacy.org

The Coalition for the Advancement of Medical Research is a nonpartisan, pro–stem cell research coalition of more than one hundred nationally recognized patient organizations, universities, scientific groups, and foundations. CAMR advocates

for scientific advancement in medical and health research that will provide cures for a number of different diseases, such as cancer, diabetes, Alzheimer disease, heart disease, Parkinson's disease, and spinal cord injuries. The coalition has worked to educate lawmakers on the importance of stem cell research and to advocate for stem cell research funding and against legislation that will limit stem cell research meant to provide cures for disease.

Do No Harm: The Coalition of Americans for Research Ethics
1100 H St. NW, Suite 700, Washington, DC 20005
(202) 347-6840 • fax: (202) 347-6849
e-mail: media@stemcellresearch.org
Web site: www.stemcellresearch.org

Do No Harm is a national coalition of scientists, researchers, health-care professionals, bioethicists, and legal professionals dedicated to the development of medical treatments and therapies that do not rely on embryonic stem cell research. The coalition strives to educate and inform policy makers and the public regarding the ethical issues relevant to the stem cell debate. On a legislative front, the coalition advocates for the continuation of federal laws prohibiting the federal funding of embryonic stem cell research. Do No Harm's Web site features the latest news about adult and umbilical cord stem cell research from around the world and provides commentary on the moral and ethical objections to using human embryos for scientific research.

The Heritage Foundation
214 Massachusetts Ave. NE, Washington, DC 20002
(202) 546-4400 • fax: (202) 546-8328
e-mail: info@heritage.org
Web site: www.heritage.org

The Heritage Foundation is a conservative think tank dedicated to formulating and promoting conservative public policies based on the principles of free enterprise, limited govern-

ment, individual freedom, and strong national defense. They have published "Federal Stem Cell Research," an article that assembles a diverse group of experts to discuss the issue of federal funding for embryonic stem cell research, and "Tough Cell," a commentary that expresses opposition to any federal funding of stem cell research.

International Society for Stem Cell Research (ISSCR)
111 Deer Lake Road, Suite 100, Deerfield, IL   60015
(847) 509-1944 • fax: (847) 480-9282
e-mail: isscr@isscr.org
Web site: www.isscr.org

The International Society for Stem Cell Research is an independent, nonprofit organization established to disseminate information about stem cell research, to advocate for further research involving stem cells, and to encourage professional and public education in all areas of stem cell research and application. ISSCR publishes the *Pulse*, a newsletter that provides the latest news on stem cell research, including scientific breakthroughs. The organization also offers opinions on ethical and moral issues surrounding the topic of embryonic stem cell research, updates on stem cell legislation state-by-state and all over the world, and essays explaining the basics of embryonic stem cell research, nuclear transfer, and other controversial issues.

National Institutes of Health (NIH)
9000 Rockville Pike, Bethesda, MD   20892
(301) 496-4000
e-mail: nihinfo@od.nih.gov
Web site: www.nih.org

The National Institutes of Health is a government organization that develops, maintains, and supports scientific discoveries and innovative research strategies that will significantly protect and improve the health of U.S. citizens. The NIH disseminates medical and scientific information and conducts research into the causes, diagnosis, prevention, and cure of hu-

man diseases. The NIH Stem Cell Characterization Facility is dedicated to comparing federally approved human embryonic stem cell lines and establishing standards for all aspects of the cell-culturing process, as well as quality control and monitoring. The NIH Web site offers a number of articles on the latest scientific breakthroughs on stem cell research and clarifies federal policy on the limitation for funding embryonic stem cell research.

Stem Cell Action Network (SCAN)
Web site: www.stemcellaction.org

The Stem Cell Action Network is a grassroots, volunteer group of patients and their families and friends that came together to support federal funding for stem cell research. Arguing that embryonic stem cell research has the potential to remedy or cure Alzheimer disease, juvenile diabetes, Parkinson's disease, multiple sclerosis, amyotrophic lateral sclerosis, spinal cord injuries, and many other illnesses and injuries, SCAN organizes people affected by stem cell research and the government's ban on funding of embryonic stem cell research to take action at a grassroots level to change governmental policy. The network provides information on individual members of Congress and their records on such issues as using excess embryos from in vitro fertilization treatments for embryonic stem cell research, the nuclear transfer process, and supporting funding for stem cell research.

Student Society for Stem Cell Research (SSSCR)
e-mail: info@ssscr.org
Web site: www.ssscr.org

Founded in 2003, the Student Society for Stem Cell Research is an international network dedicated to the advancement of scientific research for cures through stem cell research. The SSSCR network spans more than ten countries and includes students, researchers, patient advocates, and policy makers dedicated to finding treatments and cures to debilitating conditions. SSSCR membership includes students from a variety

of backgrounds and educational interests utilizing their unique skills to further the development of life-saving research and the acceptance of emerging biotechnologies. They strive to organize proponents of stem cell research, help victims and their families, advance scientific progress, and move research forward by eliminating legislative barriers that hinder cures. They sponsor courses and seminars to help educate students on scientific and ethical issues surrounding stem cell research and to provide guidance in starting a local chapter of SSSCR.

Bibliography

Books

Andrea L. Bonnicksen	*Crafting a Cloning Policy: From Dolly to Stem Cells.* Washington, DC: Georgetown University Press, 2002.
Melinda Cooper	*Life as Surplus: Biotechnology and Capitalism in the Neoliberal Era.* Seattle: University of Washington Press, 2008.
John Dombrink and Daniel Hillyard	*Sin No More: From Abortion to Stem Cells, Understanding Crime, Law, and Morality in America.* New York: New York University Press, 2007.
Cynthia Fox	*Cells of Cells: The Global Race to Capture and Control the Stem Cell.* New York: Norton, 2007.
Robert P. George and Christopher Tollefson	*Embryo: A Defense of Human Life.* New York: Doubleday, 2008.
Eve Herold	*Stem Cell Wars: Inside Stories from the Frontlines.* New York: Palgrave Macmillan, 2006.
Ann A. Kiessling and Scott C. Anderson	*Human Embryonic Stem Cells: An Introduction to the Science and Therapeutic Potential.* Sudbury, MA: Jones and Bartlett, 2003.

Kristen Renwick Monroe, Ronald B. Miller, and Jerome S. Tobis, eds.	*Fundamentals of the Stem Cell Debate: The Scientific, Religious, Ethical, and Political Issues.* Berkeley and Los Angeles: University of California Press, 2008.
National Institutes of Health	*Stem Cells: Scientific Progress and Future Research Directions.* Washington, DC: National Institutes of Health, 2005.
Ann B. Parson	*The Proteus Effect: Stem Cells and Their Promise for Medicine.* Washington, DC: Joseph Henry, 2004.
Ted Peters	*The Stem Cell Debate.* Minneapolis: Fortress, 2007.
Michael Ruse and Christopher A. Pynes, eds.	*The Stem Cell Controversy: Debating the Issues.* Amherst, NY: Prometheus, 2006.
Stewart Sell	*Stem Cells Handbook.* Totowa, NJ: Humana, 2004.
Nancy E. Snow, editor	*Stem Cell Research: New Frontiers in Science and Ethics.* Notre Dame, IN: University of Notre Dame Press, 2003.
Brent Waters and Ronald Cole-Turner, eds.	*God and the Embryo: Religious Voices on Stem Cells and Cloning.* Washington, DC: Georgetown University Press, 2003.

Periodicals

Peter Aldhous	"Transformed: The Stem Cell Breakthrough," *New Statesman*, May 3, 2008.
American Spectator	"No, the Stem Cell Debate Is Not Over," April 2008.
Julian Baggini	"Now Let the Real Battle Begin," *New Statesman*, May 26, 2008.
Gary Bauer	"Breakthrough Research Vindicates Bush's Stem Cell Stance," *Human Events*, December 10, 2007.
Sharon Begley	"What Condition Could Stem Cells Help First?" *Newsweek*, July 7, 2008.
Richard Brookhiser	"Matters over Morality," *Time*, August 6, 2007.
Chap Clark	"Stem Cell Choices," *Sojourners*, April 2007.
Michael F. Clarke and Michael W. Becker	"Stem Cells: The Real Culprits in Cancer?" *Scientific American*, June 2008.
Nancy Gibbs	"Wanted: Someone to Play God," *Time*, March 3, 2008.
A.C. Grayling	"Pro-life and Anti-ethics," *New Scientist*, December 27, 2007.
Stephen S. Hall	"Crossing the Lines," *Discover*, October 2007.

Michael Humphrey	"Advances Don't Quell Stem Cell Debate," *National Catholic Reporter*, January 11, 2008.
Celeste Kennel-Shank	"Stem Cells and Human Dignity," *Sojourners*, March 2008.
Michael Kinsley	"Mine Is Longer than Yours," *New Yorker*, April 7, 2008.
Sarah Kliff	"A Stem-Cell Surprise," *Newsweek*, July 30, 2007.
Robert Langreth and Matthew Herper	"Stem Cells Get Real," *Forbes*, June 16, 2008.
Robin McKie	"Religion Must Not Block Progress," *New Statesman*, May 19, 2008.
Neil Munro	"Two Roads on Stem Cell Policy," *National Journal*, August 4, 2007.
National Review	"Stem Cell Success," December 17, 2007.
New Scientist	"Still No Substitute for Embryonic Stem Cells," May 3, 2008.
Karen Rowan	"Tearing Down the Stem Cell Wall," *Discover*, April 2008.
Jane Swift	"Donated Eggs Don't Come Cheap," *New Scientist*, December 8, 2007.

Index